FIRMLY PLANTED PUBLICATIONS
An imprint of Equipped for Life Ministries, Dallas, Texas

I0211176

A Shrinking World Requires a Better Christianity

B. Dale Taliaferro

A Shrinking World Requires a Better Christianity
Published by Firmly Planted Publications
An imprint of Equipped for Life Ministries

Cover Art by Hannah Gleghorn Design, Frisco, Texas

Printed copies also sold at Logos Book Store, 6620 Snider Plaza, Dallas, Texas, 75205-3483

Scripture quotations taken from the New American Standard Bible®, Copyright © 1960, 1962, 1963, 1968, 1971, 1972, 1973, 1975, 1977, 1995 by The Lockman Foundation (www.Lockman.org). Used by permission.

For information:
Equipped for Life Ministries
P.O. Box 12013
Dallas, Texas 75225
U.S.A.

Library of Congress Number:

First Edition / First Printing / 2019

Other Books by B. Dale Taliaferro

The Love of God Series

This series takes the reader step by step through the process of rethinking the theology that he has been taught and comparing it to the Biblical texts used to support it. There are six short volumes in this series, each volume building upon the previous one. As a result, they must be read in order to keep from missing the arguments given for the positions being taken. Those arguments are not repeated in each volume. Volume one, for example, will give the rationale for justification and for how it must be distinct from salvation. Those arguments will not be repeated in volume two even though volume two demonstrates the truth of the positions taken in volume one. The six volumes are as follows:

The Prodigal Paradigm, the Bible's Real Storyline

Acceptable to God without being Saved? Saul was! Could others be today?

The Grand Spiritual Assumption, is salvation really about heaven?

Freedom through the Cross, the Cross in God's Plan

The Offer of a Second Inheritance, and a life to obtain it

Road to Heaven?   Constructed by Men Alone

This book is a response to Dr. Robert Jeffress' book, Not All Roads Lead to Heaven, which presents the classic Christian view of who is able to obtain heaven and how. In my response I demonstrate that no one needs to believe in Jesus in order to get to heaven. The Bible is not about finding a road to heaven. It is about walking with the God who placed you on earth.

Living through Crises

This book illustrates the extraordinary life that Jesus gives to all who believe Him for it.

Living through Crises Leader's Guide

Through a series of questions with the answers given, the reader is taught to personalize the principles in the main book.

Living through Crises Study Guide

This book offers some of the questions that are covered in the Leader's Guide for the student to fill in before discussing them in the small group.

Judas and Divine Grace, revised edition

The proofs are given herein that Judas had believed in Jesus, had received eternal life, had followed Jesus faithfully, and will be in the coming Kingdom of Messiah.

Table of Contents

Preface

My goal in this book is to set forth some of the necessary applications that the conclusions from this study series force upon us. If we have drawn the correct conclusions on justification, salvation, eternal life, the kingdom of heaven, and forgiveness, those studies lead us to these applications. It is time we make a huge change in our approach to the world around us.

Everyone can easily test what has been written in the preceding five volumes not by checking with his favorite theologian but by taking out a concordance and looking up every use of the key words that we have been studying together, noting the breadth of their possible meanings and the contextual limitation of those meanings in each passage. If you are not equipped to study the use of these words in the Bible, then go to your church and ask the leaders to offer the congregation a class on hermeneutics. You will be asking for a course that will teach you the principles and practice of interpretation so you can test what everyone is saying to you.

If you can't obtain a good, objective, non-theological study in hermeneutics from your church, then contact Western Seminary in Portland, Oregon and ask them to send you or make available to you through the internet Dr. Earl Radmacher's class that he taught for over 35 years on hermeneutics. A shorter approach has been printed in a book by The Timothy Initiative on hermeneutics. This abridged book was edited by Dr. Radmacher so it will include the basics of the class he taught at the seminary level. Don't be afraid that such a class will be beyond your grasp. All the seminary students at Western had to take this class the first year of their seminary studies regardless of the degree program that they had entered. I remember knowing nothing when I first took it. That class has become the foundation of my ministry for the last 47 years. I *may* be only slightly off base to say that it was the most important class I took in seminary.

My problem was that I too had placed my trust in men. They were so much more scholarly than I was or ever hoped to be. I was so fortunate to have these men teach me. I would never have thought to question their views any more than I would have reason to question their character.

I *assumed* that what had been taught for over five hundred years by some of the best scholars the church has ever produced couldn't be wrong. I *assumed* that what I had been taught was thoroughly Biblical in its formulation. I *assumed* the references to all the verses, which were used to prove the understanding being set forth, were accurate interpretations of those verses. I *assumed* that scholarship meant practical infallibility.

When our understanding changes, the applications of that new understanding will require us to see the world around us very differently. Hopefully that new perspective will lead us to be less judgmental and more loving to a world that needs to see in us the difference that Jesus makes.

I pray that God will help you, as He is helping me, to give up every dearly held belief when the Bible *explicitly* demands it. I have been blinded by the unbiblical teachings I had been taught. Have you? It is time to trust Jesus for the salve that restores a person's spiritual sight.[1] The world is about to take on a whole new look for you!

---

[1] Rev. 3:17-18.

Introduction

The world *is* shrinking, not materially, of course, but ethnically. Your neighbors are no longer just like you. They may be from India, China, Iran, or Brazil. They may be Hindis, Muslims, Baha'is, Mormons, Israelis, or Buddhists. Instead of living next to the Smiths or Jones, we may have Kumars, Lis, Wongs, Beridzes, Singhs, Cohens, or the Suzukis[1] next door. Many of them are very open to the Christians' message about Jesus and what He is offering them freely.

But a good many of them are terribly offended by the approach that some Christians take in sharing their faith, an approach not dissimilar to that of some Messianic Jews during the time the NT was being written. Basically that message was, "Unless you become like us in our beliefs and in our practices, you can never be ultimately saved by the Messiah."[2]

Not only is the approach offensive at times, the message is also distorted to demand things that Jesus never required nor would He even condoned at any time, much less today nearly two thousand years after it was first given. The real problem is that this distorted message is the only message that the Christian church has heard for the last five hundred years. So, to hear any other message raises vociferous opposition from within each person being challenged. The Christian church is now in the mode of supporting error rather than the truth. Almost one hundred per cent of these Christians are unaware of their plight. We have all

---

[1] Common names from India, China, China, Georgia (the one in Europe!), India, Israel, and Japan, respectively.
[2] Acts 15:1-11; Gal. 1:6-9; 2:1-5, 11-21; 3:1-24; 5:1-12; etc.

heard one message so often that we are convinced that it has to be true, and every other message has to be false. In short, we have all been programmed. It is devastating that the central message of Christianity is what is in error.

Do people need to be *converted* to Christianity in order to go to heaven?

Do they need to *believe in Jesus* in order to be forgiven of their sins?

Does belief in Jesus offer *the only pathway to heaven*?

Is all the world doomed for hell except for Christians?

Do you think those questions might be at least a little offensive if the shoe was on the other foot? The radical Muslims believe that only they will enter paradise, and everyone else will go to hell. Their way is the only way. Isn't that exactly what the Christian message is as well?

But *what if* that whole discussion is beside the main point of Jesus' purpose in coming and extraneous to His central teaching?

What if Jesus' central teaching isn't about going to heaven?

What if His purpose in coming was not to provide a pathway to heaven?

What if the message is about living life well spiritually?

What if the message is about walking with the God of all creation in love and with His power?

And *what if* that walk includes both a belief system and a works system that applies those beliefs to life in daily practice?

This book is a call to radical change. Not everyone will be able to make the changes that are needed. They won't be able not because of any inability that resides within their natures, but because of the constraints of their theological convictions. All convictions restrain; some for good and some for evil, but all restrain. *Orthodox Christianity can keep a person from the truth.*

This book is to help you fight through those unbiblical restraints so that you can develop beliefs that are thoroughly Biblical. But to suggest that this will not be an enormous battle would be disingenuous. It will be the greatest battle that you have ever fought. *Let the Bible be your guide rather than what man says, including the author that you're presently reading. The Bible will not lead you astray if you take it literally and as a whole.* Meet with others who want to wrestle over the issues in order to come to Biblical conclusions. May your study prove to be successful, enabling you to better live the life Jesus desires to give you moment by moment.

Section One

What Needs to be Better?

Chapter 1

The Need to be Better at
Manifesting our Distinctiveness

At the top of the list of things that need to be better within Christianity is the display or manifestation of the life that Jesus gives to all who believe in Him. Christians need to actually *live* the life that Jesus gives them instead of merely *possessing* it with the hope that it will, somehow, guarantee them, in the vernacular of orthodox Christianity, a home with God in heaven.

This life is unique. In fact, no other religion in the world offers such a wonder as this life is. But the profoundly sad reality is few Christians seem conversant about this life and even fewer understand how to live it. It is so attractive, as well as powerful, wise, and virtuous, that it naturally draws interest from those who observe it being lived before them. This life gives the one experiencing it resources that others simply don't possess.

I remember going to my first College Life meeting as a freshman at the University of Alabama. There were only about thirty students at the meeting, but the distinctiveness they displayed, a distinctiveness which seemed to come from the inside out, caught my attention. After four years of being connected to these fellow students, I chose the most unlikely path for the rest of my life, that of being a fulltime minister. Having studied for a medical profession, turning to a ministerial profession was more than a bit strange. What I saw in those students' lives and what I learned to live myself over those four years inspired me to imagine what the world could be like if everyone was trained in living this life. It was extraordinary then, and it continues to be extraordinary now, forty-eight years later!

Upon graduating from the University of Alabama, I joined the staff of the same group that had taught me about this extraordinary life that could be lived by anyone who learned to trust Jesus for it. My wife, whose life had also been so deeply influenced by the life that was being lived before us by the students involved in this campus ministry, was more eager than I to join this group and to dedicate our lives to sharing the simple truths about this exceptional life. It is available to all who want it. And it is available for free! There are no steps or hoops to jump through to receive it. It is absolutely free because it is provided by God Himself without cost to everyone who will trust His Son for it.

A couple of times our staff team visited other college campuses to share with the students on those campuses the life we had found to be so fulfilling. During those visits students would come up and ask us, "What makes you all so different?" You see, the difference this life makes was clearly discernible. In fact, it almost seemed to be tangible.

About the second year on staff my stepmother came to visit us on campus to see first-hand what we were doing. As she prepared to leave, after attending our campus wide outreach meeting on Sunday night, she said, "What you have is different. I have never seen anything quite like it. I'm going back to tell my church about the impact you are having with these college students. Maybe I can get them to become involved in a similar ministry to help bring some *life* to our church and youth programs." The difference, once again, continued to be discernible and as attractive as it was discernible. The Bible actually calls it the sweet aroma of

Christ[1] which is beyond a person's own adequacy to produce within.[2] You don't get it by going to church or attending a small group Bible study. You bring it with you to those meetings.

This life is unique and is available only to those who follow Jesus in faith. But, it should be obvious to everyone that *it is not automatically experienced* by anyone within the realm of Christianity. Many Christians have believed in Jesus without understanding that a walk *with* Him is a walk *by* Him *in* and *through* the one walking. If He is not the animating principle of our lives, our conformity into His image will always fall short of what God intends for us. *We become like Him only to the extent that He lives His life through us.*

In the next several sections within this chapter, I would like to break down *this life* into bite size, manageable terms. Hopefully the reader will get enough clarity and information to make *this life* his own experience. *This life is Jesus' distinctive offer.* Describing it ought to be our primary task when we share our faith to a world in need of internal renewal, refreshment, enablement, and virtue. *This life* provides all the resources that a person needs to overcome every trial that God deems wise for him to face. And, interestingly enough, *this life* is a foretaste of the life to come. This isn't heavenly truth; this is kingdom truth.

This Life Comes from Jesus

The most self-evident thing I could say for the person seeking this extraordinary life as his normal experience is that Jesus is the giver of the life that we are describing. All that a person needs to do is believe in Him, and Jesus will give him *eternal life*, the

---

[1] 2Cor. 2:14-16.
[2] 2Cor. 3:5-6.

abundant life that makes living a joy[1] as it provides a confident experience of spiritual victory over every kind of trial imaginable.[2] But maybe its most important characteristic is that it is the sure, continuous way of experiencing the love that God desires to pour out upon the one living by it.[3] *This life is available in relationship with Jesus.* It is Jesus, and Jesus alone, who is the giver of this life. Even though the Spirit may be used in the process of giving it, this life still comes from Jesus alone.[4]

This Life IS Jesus

But, as they seem to frequently say in the commercials on TV, *there is more!* The critical fact to understand here is the truth that *not only is Jesus the giver of this extraordinary life, but He is also what is given.* The life that He gives is nothing less than His own life; all that is communicable (transferable) to a human He gives whenever a person is trusting Him for it. Consequently, the Bible is replete with references to this life and to the resulting spiritual victory that is described as being *in* Christ or *through* Christ or *because of* our union *to* Christ.

Listen to how the apostle Paul described it in Col. 3:1-4:

> "If then you have been raised up with Christ, keep seeking the things above, where Christ is, seated at the right hand of God. Set you mind on the things above, not on the things that are on earth. *For you have died and your life is hidden with Christ in God.* When *Christ, who is our life*, is revealed, then you also will be revealed with Him in glory."

He is not only the giver of abundant life; He *is* the abundant life

---

1 John 15:4-5, 11.
2 Rom. 8:35-37.
3 Rom. 8:38-39.
4 John 10:27-28; 16:12-15.

that is given. This fact ought to change our view of what this life is even when it is referred to as *eternal life*. It is unfortunate that the English term *eternal* was ever used to translate the Greek term αιωνιος (transliterated as aiõnios). While this will be addressed later, for now remember that *eternal life is still identifiable as Christ's own life and nothing else*. It isn't a synonym for salvation (deliverance or rescue) from hell; it doesn't mean going to heaven when we die to be with God eternally. The life, that is given at the moment that faith is placed in Jesus, is *Christ's own life*. His life is offered to meet the seemingly endless variety of needs present in our world today.

If this life is actually Christ's life, we ought to find some references to Christ being in the one trusting in Christ. And we do. In Col. 1:27 the simple phrase occurs that says, "Christ in you, the hope of glory."[1] Christ in us to empower us;[2] Christ in us to guide us;[3] Christ in us to transform our minds;[4] Christ in us to make us adequate in all things required by God from us;[5] Christ in us to create the emotions that lift us up,[6] replacing those that cast us down and tend to crush our hearts. In short, Christ is in us to transform us into His image[7] (through the Spirit's ministry). This life is what Jesus displayed in all of His actions while on earth, the very same life that made others stand in awe. Jesus' disciples will be like Him to the extent that they reflect His life.

We are in Christ Jesus so that He can be in us in all of His

---

[1] Glory is not a reference to heaven; it is a reference to the coming kingdom of Messiah. This is seen clearly in Rom. 8:18-25 (3:23?); Heb. 2:5-9; etc.
[2] Phil. 4:13; 2Tim. 2:1.
[3] 1Cor. 2:16; Phil. 2:5; Col. 2:8; John 14:20; 15:7.
[4] Rom. 12:2; 2Cor. 3:18; 10:5.
[5] Col. 2:6-7; Eph. 4:11-13; 2Cor. 3:4-6.
[6] Cf., John 15:4-5 with John 14:27, John 15:9, and John 15:11.
[7] Rom. 8:29; Gal. 4:19; 2Cor. 3:17-18.

communicable (or transferable) fullness. All this is God's doing. He united the person who has trusted *in* Christ *to* Christ so that he could have all that Christ offers whenever he trusts Him to give it. When a person is trusting Jesus to supply his spiritual needs, Paul described that person as having Jesus actually live *through* him. He said it this way:

> "I have been crucified with Christ; and it is **no longer I who live**, but **Christ lives in me**, and the life that I now live in the flesh **I live by faith in the Son of God** who loved me and delivered Himself up for me." (Gal. 2:20, emphases mine)

There is so much here that could be profitably expounded! But for our purposes we will focus upon the three phrases that I have emphasized in the verse. There is an "I" within each person. Either that *"I" can live*, controlling, empowering, and directing the personal life, or *Christ can live within*, controlling, empowering, and directing the life. There is no automatic spirituality that a person has just because he is a Christian or because he has believed in Christ at some point in the past. Each person must choose to trust in Jesus moment by moment for *the life that Christ desires to live through him.*

While we can describe this life according to its several attributes or fruits, it is actually a package deal: all of the fruits come with the life. So, if one is drawing upon this life for his personal needs, he will have all the virtues, wisdom, and power that are inherent in the life (which is also referred to as the fruit of the Spirit in Gal. 5:22-23 because it is the Spirit who takes *from* Christ and gives it *to* us as John 16:12-15 explains).

The greatest need of the church today is to refocus upon the supernatural life of Jesus that can be lived only by accessing it by faith in a moment by moment fashion. If we are to impact the world profoundly, then we need to illustrate through our lives what is being offered to the rest of the world by Jesus. If Jesus came to give life, and we rarely manifest that life, we aren't showing the world the difference that Christ makes. As we will see, He didn't come to get anyone to heaven. He didn't come to give mankind a new set of rules to follow. He certainly didn't come to start a new religion called Christianity (which is supposed to supersede the Jewish faith of the OT). He came to carry all those who trust Him moment by moment through this life in an extraordinary, spiritual fashion. If we aren't expressing that life, the world will continue to question the difference in our faith and theirs. And for very good reasons! If our faith is not livable, what good is it, practically speaking?

This Life Takes us beyond our own Abilities

The power of this life will be clear when we experience how it takes us beyond the point where our natural, unaided abilities under the control of indwelling sin leave us. Who hasn't tried to overcome a bad habit or a shortcoming only to fail time after time? In Rom. 7:14—8:6, the apostle Paul explains that what man cannot do *by the flesh*,[1] he is more than capable of doing by the power of God's Spirit dwelling in him.[2] All the choices he wanted to make and all the actions he wanted to perform he could not accomplish if he allowed indwelling sin to be master of his soul.[3] But if he presented his members to God by faith[4] (or in the context of Rom. 7:14—8:6, if he presented his members to God by trusting in the Spirit), he would be able to give the righteous responses

---

[1] Rom. 7:14-25.
[2] Rom. 8:1-6.
[3] Rom. 6:12-14.
[4] Rom. 6:12-13.

15

that God required, responses that he himself desired to give. Such a life, Paul was comforted to know, God would *never condemn*.[1] Such a walk God would *always justify* because His Spirit produced it. Whatever God does, He, obviously, must justify. As Christ lives His life through the person trusting Him for that life, that person must receive God's approval, God's justification, since it is His Son producing the responses that are being given. Jesus always does what pleases the Father.

When some requirement of God seems out of reach, when it seems too high to achieve, when it seems to ask too much, when it appears to ask more than you know you have to give, it is nevertheless possible through God's Spirit. For example, you realize that you have been commanded to love your neighbor. You have tried and tried to love him. But he has only become more ornery than appreciative in the process. The amazing thing is that you can still fulfill God's righteous command by walking in dependence upon God's Spirit[2] who will produce the love within for you to display outwardly. You don't need to produce the love; you only need to use the love that is being produced. By faith you know that love was part of the life given to you to live by. Now you step out, trusting in the flow of love from the life within.

There is probably not a person alive who hasn't thought, at one time or another, that he couldn't do what the Bible was asking him to do. As a result, he withheld *forgiveness* knowing that he was clearly commanded by God to forgive.[3] *Anxiety* has become

---

[1] Rom. 8:1. When the debate over the purpose of Paul in writing the book of Romans is renewed in the coming years, as I suspect it will be, it will be found out that the entire argument of the whole book of Romans supports the inclusion of the second half of verse one which should read, (There is therefore now no condemnation for those who are in Christ Jesus) "who do not walk according to the flesh, but according to the Spirit."

[2] Lev. 19:18; Rom. 13:9 and Rom. 8:4; Lk. 10:25-28; Gal. 5:13-17.

[3] Eph. 4:31-32; Matt. 6:14-15.

an unwelcome but common companion although it is clearly forbidden.[1] All kinds of *fears* are entertained[2] except for the one that is urged upon us as the panacea for the others.[3] *Depression* is tolerated and excused when God has given a solution for it.[4] *Anger* has become a common, almost acceptable, response to disappointment or hurt[5] even though God warns us that anger and angry people must be shunned; it/they can lead to trouble now[6] and can never achieve the righteousness of God.[7]

In short, our continuing spiritual failures are all too obvious. We've become content to listen to the promises of those who don't understand the power of the spiritual life that Jesus gives. They have, at the very best, given us *a coping mechanism*, but not *a life* that can overcome the trials that face us.

In addition to all of these pitfalls, there is a *lack of peace* that leaves the soul in a state of turmoil by default. There is a growing *impatience* that cannot evade one's notice. *Kindness* has almost disappeared altogether, and the topic of *self-control* is no longer discussed because there is no agreement upon a standard to which a person ought to conform. That is the reality most of us can relate to immediately. And unfortunately, that reality uncovers the real condition or state of our own hearts. We are trapped in Romans seven, and we can't see a way out.

So, when Jesus offers a person *His* peace, *His* joy, *His* love, *His* power, *His* wisdom and knowledge,[8] and *His* perspective on the

---

[1] Phil. 4:6-7.
[2] Prov. 29:25.
[3] Ex. 20:20; Gen. 20:11; Acts 10:34-35.
[4] Prov. 12:25 and Ps. 38:18 give the solution for depression when 1John 1:9 is fulfilled.
[5] Gen. 4:6-7; Eph. 4:31-32.
[6] Prov. 22:24-25; Eph. 4:26-27.
[7] Js. 1:19-20.
[8] John 14:26-27, John 15:11, John 15:9-10 and Rom. 8:38-39, Eph. 1:18-23, Col. 2:2-3 and Js. 1:5-8, respectively.

central purpose and meaning to life,[1] such an offer can't help but be attractive to all men in every nation. Are you experiencing this kind of life today? It clearly is what God is offering to each one of us. The God who created us knows our capacities and our needs. *His commands indirectly reveal our capacities and His promises address and cover all of our needs.*

These are the virtues that are the most needed and the vices that are most in need of overcoming. Regardless of how long some sins have dominated us, the power of Jesus Christ to free us from those captivating sins is closer to us than we can imagine. As Jesus works through us, He addresses and overcomes the sin that so easily entangles us[2] and the sins that flow from that entangling indwelling sin. As a result, our greatest need is to learn how to draw the life Jesus is offering us into our present experience.

When we learn how to do that, our adequacy is not *from ourselves.* Rather our adequacy is *from Him*[3] moment by moment. Of course, God's grace is always sufficient.[4] But if a person doesn't know how to draw upon that grace, it is useless even though it may be so close and so easily accessible. Learn how to draw upon the Lord. Then do it and be free.

In the beginning of my ministry experience, I learned an easy two step method for drawing upon the life that I already possessed from the moment of my initial faith in Jesus. It can be remembered by two words: *a command,* and *a promise.* God actually *commands* us to live this marvelously astounding life. Consequently, we know it is God's will that we live by this life if He commands us to do it, right?

---

[1] Matt. 22:34-40; Lk. 10:25-28. Cf., Eccl. 12:13-14.
[2] Heb. 12:1-2.
[3] 2Cor. 3:5-6.
[4] 2Cor. 12:7-9.

In 1John 5:14-15, the apostle John says,

> "And this is the confidence which we have before Him, that, if we ask anything according to His will, He hears us. And if we know that He hears us in whatever we ask, we know that we have the requests that we have asked from Him."

God has *promised* to grant the prayer requests that are in accordance with His will. If He commands us to live by the life Jesus gives, and if we ask for that life believing that He will give what He promises to give, then we can have the confidence that we have it. *God cannot lie; He fulfills the promise of granting life to the one who follows Jesus,*[1] *seeking it from Him by faith.*[2]

It is easy to see the place faith has in all of this. One must believe that God will give what He promises to give. And then with confidence, he must believe that when he attempts to use the life that was promised to him, it is present within for his experience. The love, that Jesus is being trusted to provide, will be present; the ability to forgive will be present; the patience that is needed will be present. All that is needed will be present in the life that has been promised regardless of any emotions to the contrary.

Faith must not be dependent upon the emotions that are present. Faith believes God who in faithfulness will provide what He has promised.[3] Surprisingly, the contrary emotions, if any should exist, will eventually change without any attempt to change them. That too is a God thing! You should give thanks even when you are *not* thankful! You should rejoice even though there is *no* joy springing up from within. If you respond in faith by Jesus' life, your emotions will change as a result of God working within.

Our most basic problem today is that we don't really know

---

[1] John 10:27-30.
[2] Matt. 7:7-11.
[3] Cf., Rom. 4:19-21; 1Thess. 5:23-24.

how to walk by faith. We don't know how to trust Jesus to give to us what He has promised to produce in us for our experience. There is no end to the professional experts that continually promise us the mirage of meaning, purpose, and fulfillment. Their illusionary oasis is as heartbreaking as it is inviting.

Maybe the most common mistake is to assume that a moral response is a godly response. Many suppose that doing the right thing is all that God requires of us. But it isn't. We are to do whatever it is that God has told us to do from a love for Him[1] and by a faith in Him.[2] Otherwise we are building a house upon the sand which is unable to stand in times of trial.[3] The difference in a moral action and a spiritual action is that a spiritual action is not only doing the God ordained thing, but it also has the ability to raise up all those impacted by it to a dependence upon God. If our obedience doesn't point one to God as it is supposed to,[4] how can others grow by watching our walk with God? A moral act does not produce spiritual results. Only a spiritual act produces spiritual results.

This is the life that we must manifest to the world as we share the difference that Jesus can make. All that a person needs can be found in the *life* that He freely offers to all men who trust in Him. This life is the solution to all of man's inadequacies. Live by it and conquer the situations that you must face.

---

[1] Rev. 2:1-7.
[2] Heb. 11:6; Rom. 14:23.
[3] Matt. 7:24-27; Lk. 6:46-49.
[4] Matt. 5:16.

Chapter 2

The Need to be Better at
Understanding the Universal Will of God

The standard that we measure others by is our own understanding of the requirements set forth in the Bible. If they don't follow our Scriptures, *as we understand them*, then they are out of the will of God. If the disagreements are large enough, then we have the tendency to separate from them altogether. But what if our present interpretation of our own Bibles is in error? Are we brave enough to critique our own understanding?

Most of us have said some pretty derogatory statements about others with whom we disagree within the Christian faith. This tendency to ridicule and despise the position of others only increases when other religions are involved. We suppose that the whole world is on thin ice, that is, everyone except us.

Does God need to send each nation an anthology of revelation containing thirty-nine books (as God did for the Jewish people of the OT)? Does He need to send each nation a canon of sacred Scriptures containing twenty-seven books or sixty-six books of instruction (as God did for the those who trusted in Jesus as Messiah)? Is all that revelation needed to explain to the people of a given nation what His will is and to what standard of behavior they will be held accountable?

These thoughts naturally lead to further questions: "Does God's revelation to other nations need to be exactly the same as what He has already communicated in written form to us? Can

He also communicate through spiritual leaders, directly to individuals, or through nature sufficiently for them to live in a way that pleases Him?" We must also face the fact that those privileged nations, to whom God has given His written revelation, have not greatly benefited from those written guidelines that they received from God. Only a small portion of them, it seems, actually devote themselves to humbly studying and obediently following the revelation that has been given to them. We may have more secure, written truth than others, but has that truth secured in us a life of righteousness that pleases God?

If Jesus could summarize the entire requirements of the Jewish Scriptures, all thirty-nine books of revelation, into two commands, and He did,[1] don't you think it is possible that God could communicate to other nations and other peoples the same summarized message without writing it down for them in all of its details? If they *fear God* and *do what is right*, they will be acceptable to God[2] just as much as the Jews could have been if they attempted to follow all thirty-nine books of revelation that they possessed.

It naturally follows then that the Gentiles around the world, who are without the written revelation of God, and the Jews, who had been given God's revelation in written form, will be just as acceptable to God if they fulfill those two, divine requirements[3] that Jesus gave them. Likewise, if you and I follow the New Testament revelation that has been given to us by Jesus and His apostles, we will be no more acceptable to God than those who simply follow the two commands given by Jesus.

I am well aware of the spiritual heartburn that these

---

[1] Matt. 22:34-40
[2] Acts 10:34-35.
[3] Cf., John 9:31.

statements create in the souls of some Christians. That turmoil is created simply because the orthodox theology of Christianity is at a loss when it attempts to reconcile passages like Acts 10:34-35 with its historical belief that faith in Jesus is needed to be rightly related to God. It is clear that these two viewpoints can't be harmonized regardless of the circumlocution that might be used. The exclusivity of Christianity, which is based upon taking John 14:6 and Acts 4:12 out of their immediate contexts, should be rejected. But we will get to that discussion soon enough.

I recently saw a new survey that the Barna group took and analyzed.[1] And after reading their analyzes, I came to the conclusion that the Barna group needs to re-read and restudy the Bible for themselves. Their plumb line for what is correct and what is heresy is unbiblical. You read that correctly. The Barna group's basis for giving *correct* answers is *man's theology*, rather than the Word of God.

For example, the Barna group adheres to the dominate Christian belief that not all people pray to the same God even though their survey registered twenty-eight per cent of the responders believe otherwise. David, the most spiritual king that Israel ever had and the one to whom God compared all other kings, wrote:

> "O Thou who dost hear *prayer, to Thee all men come (to pray)*." (Ps. 65:2)

Such an idea certainly fits with *the universalism* entreated repeatedly in the Scriptures.[2] It also fits with the fact that all the nations belong to God.[3] That is the reason that He is rightly described as

---

[1] https://www.barna.com/research/competing-worldviews-influence-todays-christians/.
[2] E.g., Ps. 66:1; 67:1-7; 72:1-11; 94:9-10; 100:1-5; 117:1-2; 148:7, 11-13; 150:6. This entreaty will be fulfilled in the future when all people will worship the God of Israel (e.g., Ps. 22:27-28; 66:1-4; 138:4-5; 145:21; Phil. 2:8-11; Rev. 5:11-14).
[3] Ps. 82:8.

the God of all men.[1] He is the creator and sustainer of all men, communicating continuously with them and drawing them all into a closer relationship with Himself. Even though Jesus enlightens all men coming into the world,[2] they are not all responding equally well to His illuminations.

The survey sadly acknowledged that nearly one out of three Christians believe that "if you do good, you will receive good, and if you do bad, you will receive bad." The Barna group would have Christendom believe that holding such "a karmic view" of life is unbiblical. But the Bible *explicitly* says that whatever a man sows that is what he shall also reap.[3]

The context of Paul's sowing and reaping metaphor warns a person that if he sows to the flesh (i.e., does something bad, produces something fleshly or sinful), he will reap something bad (corruption). But the context also assures a person that if he sows to the Spirit (i.e., does something good from God's Spirit), he will reap eternal life.[4] That certainly sounds like "do good, get good; do bad, get bad" to me.

There are multitudes of verses throughout the OT that affirm this same truth.[5] The entire doctrine of rewards teaches this principle.[6] If a person does what God asks him to do, the way God asks him to do it, God will reward him for it. If he refuses to do what God has asked him to do, he will receive a negative *recompense* (a negative pay back) from Jesus at the Judgment Seat of

---

[1] Rom. 3:29-30.
[2] John 1:9.
[3] Gal. 6:7-8.
[4] One of many verses that demonstrates the traditional view of eternal life is inadequate.
[5] Isn't this idea the basic point of the whole book of Proverbs? Isn't this the prayer of David in Ps. 28:4, 6-8? Isn't the doctrine of judgment according to works based upon this very premise (cf., Eccl. 12:13-14; Dan. 12:1-2; Matt. 16:24-27; Rom. 14:10-12; 2Cor. 5:10)?
[6] Cf., e.g., Matt. 6:1-24; 1Cor. 3:9-15.

Christ. But if you fear God reverentially now, you won't have to fear His discipline in the judgment.

Now we all agree that such a view describes life in general. God can overrule that cause and effect as often as He deems wise. But, generally speaking, if you sow bad acts, you will reap bad consequences. If you sow good deeds, you will be blessed.[1]

Although over half the Christians surveyed strongly agree that the Bible teaches that God will help those who help themselves, the Barna group judges this to be another evidence of unbiblical perspectives creeping into and distorting a truly Christian worldview. But, just to mention one more passage, we ought to turn to Ps. 37:40 which says,

> "And the **Lord helps** them, and delivers them; He delivers them from the wicked, and saves them, *because they* take refuge in Him."

The entire Bible is clear that God never seeks obedience or conformity from men without also requiring faith in Him in the process.[2] So, I am saying that God helps those who help themselves by seeking refuge in Him. If they do that, God will certainly deliver them from the wicked and their wicked plans. In other words, God is saying, "Do this, and good will come. Don't do this and be exposed to the wickedness of evil men without any refuge." Additionally, there are several conditions that must be fulfilled for a person to take refuge in God like Bible study, prayer, and worship. All must be done in faith as previously stated if God is to be pleased.

All of this is to make the simple point that the Bible, not some Christian tradition or historic, orthodox perspective, is the true

---

[1] Cf., 2Pet. 3:10-12.
[2] Cf., Ps. 119:1-2; Heb. 11:6. Hebrews 11 is describing how all the people in the OT had to live in order to please God, and without faith it was impossible to please Him.

plumb line for all beliefs. If we would become more Biblical in our thinking, we would not be so restrained in our actions. And those who don't have the Bible should not panic because God is communicating to all men exactly what He will hold them responsible for both in this life and at the judgment after this life is over. We need to know that those nations who do not have or do not follow our Bible may be, nevertheless, perfectly acceptable to God before we ever share Jesus with them. How so? Because they are already responding to the revelation that God has been giving them.

The Scriptures do set forth a universal will of God. This is simply the bottom line, so to speak, of God's requirements for a person to be acceptable to Him. In the nature of the case, God's universal will must be available to all men. What would the content of that universal will be?

What Exactly is God's Universal Will?

This is one of the most intriguing studies you will undertake if you are open to the teachings of the Bible. It will also be one of the most disturbing studies you will engage in because it will go counter to all that you have been taught as you made historic, orthodox Christianity your plumb line of truth for acceptance with God. You will find that God is actually a great deal more gracious and merciful, and compassionate and caring than what we were taught, assuming that you are willing to examine the ramifications of what you have been taught. But such openness is not typically found in many Christian groups.

Our first concern, generally speaking, is discovering how a given teaching affects us personally. If it affects us in a positive way, we don't consider with a lot of compassion all those who may be affected by the same teaching in a very negative way. If it is good for us, we generally don't spend much time considering what it is saying about others less fortunate than we are.

So, for example, if we have been taught that we should pray in the name of Jesus for our prayers to be heard by God, we are likely to conclude that all those, throughout the whole world who have never heard the name of Jesus, have no access to God through prayer. How can they pray in the name of Jesus if they have never heard of Jesus?

But we aren't really disturbed by that ramification because it doesn't affect our own situation in the least. Their conundrum is overshadowed and lost sight of by our own relief that we are not like they are. Our abundance desensitizes us to their spiritual plight. Our spiritual heritage deadens us to their spiritual poverty. Do we really care about the rest of the world?

In the same way, if we have been taught that the Bible is the revealed will of God and to walk with God we must walk according to its precepts, we may be likely to concluded that those who either don't have God's Word or who don't believe that the Bible is the revelation of the will of God can't possibly walk with God. *Without a Bible to follow, the righteousness of God simply can't be obtained in practicality.* Or so we may be prone to think.

Interestingly enough, that conviction is the very one that Paul's Messianic Jewish opponents in the NT promoted. Paul spent two whole books, Galatians and Romans, demonstrating the fallacy of that conviction. *A righteous life can be lived without having a Bible as one's guide.* That, at least, was Paul's conviction.

It is easy to focus upon how we are positively guided and benefited by the revelation that God has given to us in the Bible. It is even easier to suppose that those who do not have any access to the revelation we have from God must be greatly and negatively affected by that void. From these two truths, we are likely to draw the wrong conclusions about the state or condition of the rest of the world. The privileges, that we in the West have, ought not to be held against the rest of the world who do not have them. Would it make God a respecter of persons if He judged the whole world based upon what we have rather than upon what each person has? Of course it would![1]

If God's house is a house of prayer for all mankind,[2] and it is clearly revealed to be such in both Testaments,[3] do we conclude that all men must come to it with the same doctrines and understanding of God that we have in order for them to be heard? *When God has not revealed Himself in the same way and to the same extent to all people, why should we expect all people to come to God the way we do and with our understanding?* Our God is bigger than that! He is more merciful and gracious than that! His compassion, loving-kindness, and faithfulness are broader than that as we are about to see repeatedly taught throughout the Scriptures!

The universal will of God has been revealed and must be accepted by even the most enlightened persons. Let me walk you through the *explicit*, Scriptural statements of His requirements for all people. We begin with a statement out of a book that is generally taken to be the earliest book written in the Scriptures, the book of Job.

Job, a unique man by God's own accounting

If you are not familiar with Job 1:8, you ought to read the entire first chapter to get a grasp of the immediate context. God and

---

[1] Rom. 2:11-13; 3:29-31.
[2] 1Kgs. 8:22ff; Isa. 56:7.
[3] Matt. 21:13.

28

Satan were having a little dialogue in heaven. God asked Satan what he had been doing. He responded by saying that he had been roaming about upon the earth.[1] The apostle Peter told us almost two thousand years later what Satan does when he is walking about on the earth: he is seeking someone to devour![2]

Knowing Satan and knowing what he had been up to, God asked him what he thought about His servant Job. It is nice to be noticed, but not when it can lead to the destruction of your life and the loss of everything you have, except for your complaining wife! But that is what God did. He asked Satan that while he had been down on earth, had he come across His servant Job? If he had had the chance to observe him, what was his evaluation of him?

Without going into too much detail, God explained why He was picking Job out from the others that Satan might have come across while he was walking around upon the earth. By God's own evaluation, Job was an extraordinary man with an exemplar faith. God described Job this way:

> "For there is *no one like him* upon the earth, a *blameless* and *upright* man, *fearing* God and *turning away* from evil." (Job 1:8, emphases mine)

God told Satan that Job was unique: there was no one else on earth like him! He was one of a kind. No one else had his virtuous character; no one else had his spiritual life. The two character descriptions, given in Job 1:8, being *blameless* and *upright*, may be easily seen to have flowed from his two spiritual traits, *fearing God and turning away from evil* because one of the basic truths of the whole Bible is the fact that moral virtue is grounded in spiritual

---

[1] Job. 1:7.
[2] 1Pet. 5:8.

life. Consequently, irreligion is connected to unrighteousness[1] even though the irreligious are fully aware that they are breaking God's laws of morality. On the other hand, the virtues in Job's life are traced back to his relationship with the God whom he obeyed. It is these two spiritual traits, *fearing God and turning away from evil*, that should arrest our attention.

Job feared God, and he turned away from evil. Or to say this positively, *Job feared God and did what was right*. His fear of God did not paralyze him; it exalted God and gave Job the foundation that he needed to turn away from sin and do what was right. What is right is always what God has revealed to be such. While He does not give everyone the same amount of revelation, He does require the same righteousness of life from all.

We will find that *fearing* God and *loving* God are used interchangeably throughout the Scriptures. In addition, doing what is right is often stated as obeying God, or being blameless, or being righteous. *But those two traits constitute the standard that God is requiring from all men regardless of the amount of revelation that they have been given.* All men are to fear/love God and do what is right/obey Him. That is the universal will of God for all men. While the content of the revelations that God gives may vary, it was enough to draw each person to God in order to love and obey Him. As is always the case, to whom much is given, much is require, and to whom less is given, less is required.

In passing let me make further observations relative to the place of the book of Job in our Bible. If the book of Job is the earliest book written, then it is absolutely astounding to find the concept of God that is revealed there. One would think that it should be one of the last books written because it possesses such a

---

[1] Rom. 1:18.

thorough description of the nature or attributes of God. If this was the generally known information about God at such an early age in human history, we ought to be asking, "How did it become so wide spread? From where did it originate? How could it have been so lost or distorted as time went by? Or was it?"

Apparently, all men started out well instructed on the nature and the general will of God. But through their own choices they exchanged the glory of God for vain and worthless conceptions of deity just as Paul tells us in Rom. 1:18-28. In doing so, they acted just like sheep straying from their Shepherd. They departed from Him and His will just as a prodigal might do even though he had previously known the goodness of his caregiver.

Job feared God and did what was right. By developing those two spiritual traits, He was approved by God and described as blameless and upright. He was living a life that pleased God. It should be noticed that there are a lot of elements missing from this description of Job that we *assume* are necessary and always present in the life of people rightly related to God in the OT. At this point, I urge the reader to be impressed with the simplicity of the revelation that has been given to us.

Abraham and Abimelech Together Reveal it

Even though the episode of Abraham and Abimelech occurred before the Law had been given, it is extremely interesting how the chosen one of God, Abraham, and the King of Gerar, who was completely outside of the line of people that God was giving special interest to, had so much in common. But what they had in common was not discernable until they came together. As it turns out, the motivation and guide for each of their lives was the one true God who was working in both of them.

31

After Abraham had left Haran behind and was moving around within the land of Canaan, he came finally to Gerar. But he was frightened of the ruler of Gerar, King Abimelech. He was afraid that there was no fear of his God in that king or within his kingdom.[1]

I can understand Abraham's fears. Why should he think that there would be a fear of *his* God in that place? This king and his nation were not connected in any way with the line of Shem that God had singled out after changing the languages of the peoples building the tower of Babel and dispersing them over the earth.[2] How would this King even know about Abraham's God at all? Why would he not be implacably opposed to Abraham's faith in Elohim, the almighty God of creation? Who would have told him about Elohim at this point? Abraham's practical experience didn't give him much reason to believe anything but the worst in this situation.

To Abraham's surprise, and to most of ours in the West to this day, Abimelech had developed an extraordinary relationship with God during his lifetime. How had Abimelech come to know the true God? How had he developed such a good relationship with God on his own? There are some reasons to believe that his relationship with God might have even been better than Abraham's at the time they met.

It is no accident that the description of Abimelech and the nation over which he ruled focused upon these individual's *personal righteousness*. In the two previous chapters of Genesis, Moses, writing under the inspiration of God, made the whole episode of Lot in Sodom and Gomorrah center upon the people's *personal*

---

[1] Gen. 20:11.
[2] Gen. 11:9.

righteousness or their lack of it. God expected righteousness to be present; He held each person responsible for living righteously, and because those cities had no righteous people in them, God judged them with fire and brimstone. If righteousness only comes through God's gift of it and His ability to cause it to invariably flow into the lifestyle of the person, then God is portrayed here as unrighteous in His demands, expectations, and judgment upon those cities.

The righteousness that God is seeking here is the only kind of righteousness that is found in the Bible. It is a *practical righteousness*, the virtue of right living (or the virtue of someone or something being in the right). All men are expected to have it or to be judged for not having it.

Forensic righteousness is theological speculation. Believe in it if you must, but it will not profit a person in this life or in the afterlife. It secures only a false security. Furthermore, it plainly is insufficient for entrance into the kingdom of heaven as the book of Matthew so plainly teaches.

We should also notice how closely Abimelech's question resembled the question that Abraham had asked God relative to the people of Sodom and Gomorrah. Both questions were concerned with personal, practical righteousness.

> Abraham's: "Will You [God] indeed sweep away the righteous with the wicked?"
> Abimelech's: "Will You slay a nation even though righteous?"

Abraham supposed that there were righteous people in Sodom and Gomorrah when there weren't. He obviously was not guided in his expectations by the kind of errant theology that we have assimilated into our thinking today. If Abraham believed mankind was totally depraved, he would not be expecting to find righteous people in Sodom. Rather, he would have understood immediately the reason that none would be present.

On the other hand, Abimelech spoke on behalf of himself and his own people whom he knew were righteous, a point God never contradicted. In Abraham's case, in Abimelech's, and in Abimelech's nation's case, the righteousness of God was being revealed apart from (anyone following) the Mosaic Law.[1] This is the righteousness that pleases God and the one for which man is responsible. There is no other kind of righteousness discussed in the Bible. *God does not impute in the sense of giving to a person Christ's righteousness. There is no need for such a gift since God only requires the kind of righteousness that man can give.*

It is beyond debate, if this passage is considered on its own merits objectively, that Abraham and Abimelech knew the same God even though they called Him by different names. Abraham referred to God as *Elohim*; Abimelech referred to God as *Adonai*. When Abraham's God appears to Abimelech in a dream, Abimelech instantly recognized Him as the God that he knew though by a different name than Abraham used. This God who was appearing to him in a dream was the God in whom he had been trusting. It was also Abraham's God that Abimelech's entire nation had believed in and were walking with righteously.

This does not bother *us* because *we* have an infallible guide from God that tells us that Abraham also knew the one true God as Adonai.[2] But what would we do if that information was lacking and if Abraham, for whatever reason, only referred to God as Elohim when he talked with Abimelech? What would you say about this extraordinary situation? Would you conclude that Abraham

---

[1] Rom. 3:21-22.
[2] Gen. 15:2, 8; etc.

and Abimelech did not worship and follow the same God? Would Abimelech need to be *converted* to Abraham's faith and begin calling God Elohim instead of Adonai?

When we go to Exodus three and four, we find God revealing Himself to the enslaved Israelites by *a brand-new name*, by a name that neither they nor anyone else had ever used for God before. How do you think those Israelites who had lived previously, but were now dead and buried, might have responded to belief in a God by a different name if they could speak to their fellow countrymen about entertaining belief in a God by a different name? Would they *assume* He was a different God? Or would they be open to the suggestion that this was actually the same God only now being revealed by a different name?

Is there any guidance, any application, in this passage for us today? Does God do for all people what He does for some people? Does He reveal Himself the same way to all people? The Scriptural account of the meeting between Abraham and Abimelech answers this question very plainly, "No!"

When God told Abimelech that Abraham was His prophet, Abimelech had confirmation that *his* God was also the God of Abraham. And when Abraham explained to Abimelech the reason for his deception,[1] the reason for his half-truth, he acknowledged that *his* God was also Abimelech's. *Maybe it isn't the name of God that is so important; maybe it is the nature of God that should be the focal point.* The Shakespearian line seems to be appropriate here: "What is in a name? That which we call a rose / By any other name would smell as sweet."[2] While God may be called by various names, His standard for righteousness doesn't change.

---

[1] Gen. 20:11.

[2] William Shakespeare, *Romeo and Juliet*, Act II, Scene II.

It is so apparent that Abimelech's relationship with God was genuine and intimate. When his God spoke to him in a dream, he knew it was the same God who had guided him and his nation up to this point in their lives. The concept of Biblical, practical righteousness requires a communication from God to man to which the man responds in obedience. So, to be a righteous person, and to rule over a righteous nation, there had to be constant communication from God, a communication that was gladly received and lovingly performed. It would be no surprise then that if God had appeared to Abimelech physically, he would have run up to him and would have fallen at His feet and worshipped him just like Abraham had done earlier in his life.[1]

There is no great dilemma suggested here. God had made Himself known to both men, albeit by different names. Also they both could have known God by several names, including both Elohim and Adonai. But when they came together, there was enough revelation from God to each of them for them to discern the fact that they both worshipped the same God. And the revelation was sufficient for a king to lead an entire nation righteously.

The revelation that God had given was also enough for the people of Gerar to live righteous lives. That is to say, it was enough for people to live pleasingly before the God who had revealed Himself to them. So, the questions really become, "Are we going to continue holding the rest of the world accountable for the revelation that God has given to us but which might have been withheld from them? Or will we stop merely judging the rest of the world and begin to see that God is communicating to all men? Is that not our responsibility because we have been given

---

[1] Gen. 18:1-5.

36

so much to pursue a better understanding of God and of His love for the rest of the world? Are we comprehending that God is like Christ Jesus He sent?"

We don't want to repeat the observations already given in the previous discussion of Abraham and Abimelech. But the revelation that Abimelech possessed was sufficient to lead him and his nation into a righteous walk with the God who was revealing Himself to them. The universal will of God that was present and that had been received by this King and his people was to fear God and to do what is right (or to be righteous). *The goal was to live a life that God would justify.* So, if they **feared God**, which they did, and if they **did what was right**, which they had been doing since they were described as a righteous nation, they would be acceptable to God and subject to all the blessings that He desired to pour out upon them. All of this is true without any mention of the need to have faith in a coming Messiah who would die for the sins of the world or of the need of a gift of (Christ's) righteousness that would make him acceptable to God! Can you harmonize those facts with your theological beliefs?

Moses Summarized God's Requirements

Moses reiterated and summarized God's requirements, detailed in the Law that He had given Israel about forty years earlier. According to the rabbis, His Law contained six hundred and thirteen commands and prohibitions. God permitted Moses to simplify and condense all of these instructions just before they entered the Promised Land when he said,

> "And now, Israel, what does the Lord your God require from you, but to *fear* the Lord your God, to *walk* in all His ways and *love* Him, and to *serve* the Lord your God with all your heart and with all your

37

soul, and to *keep* the Lord's commandments and His statutes which I am commanding you today for your good? Behold, to the Lord your God belong heaven and earth and *all that is in it* . . . Circumcise then your heart, and stiffen your neck no more. For the Lord your God is the God of gods and the Lord of lords . . . who executes justice for the orphan and the widow, and shows His love for the alien by giving him food and clothing. So show your *love* for the alien, for you were aliens in the land of Egypt. You shall *fear* the Lord your God; you shall *serve* Him and *cling* to Him, and you shall *swear* by His name." (Deut. 10:12-20)

God required the same things from Israel *after* the Law had been given to them as He had required from all men *before* the Law had been given. Consequently, it seems rather apparent that God gave the Law to get His chosen nation through this life in a way that pleased Him. He did not give the Law to get a person to heaven if that person would only keep the Law. Both *before* and *after* the Law was given, all were required to fear God and to do what was right by walking in His ways in love.[1] As such a walk was carried out in faith, God was pleased and, therefore, approved of all who had such a walk.[2] The Law, rather than being legal and sterile, explained how a person *clings* to God in a very close relationship.[3] Loving God and obeying Him should never be separated.[4]

The Psalms Reiterate God's Will

There are many psalms that repeat the basic theme that we are following as we proceed through the Bible and that was clearly demonstrated from Ps. 119.[5] David in Ps. 25 asks,

---

[1] Deut. 6:4-9.

[2] Heb. 11:2, 6.

[3] Ps. 119 repeatedly explains that the obedience to the Law that God was looking for was one that flowed from the heart in pursuit of God.

[4] Rev. 2:1-7.

[5] Ps. 15:1-5; 24:3-4; 33:8, 13-15, 18; 50:23; 103:17-18.

"Who is the man who *fears* the Lord? He will *instruct* him in the way he should choose. His soul will abide in prosperity, and his descendants will *inherit the land*." (Ps. 25:12-13)

Notice that he says in verses eight and ten that every Israelite who fears God will be instructed by God in the path that he should follow. So, *fearing* God and *following* His instructions lead to inheriting the land of promise.[1] This is the same standard that God had for Job, fear God and turn away from evil, and for King Abimelech and his nation, fear God and live righteously, (even though the reward for Gentiles for living such a life does not include any inheritance in the land of promise).

Even to the wicked, God gave a challenge to develop these same spiritual traits through Asaph. He touched upon them in his psalm that addressed those who forget God as they live for themselves:

"Now consider this, you who forget God, Lest I tear you in pieces, and there be none to deliver. He who *offers a sacrifice of thanksgiving* honors Me; and to him who *orders his way aright* I shall show the salvation of God." (Ps. 50:22-23, emphases mine)

Fear God by offering appropriate sacrifices, and *order your life aright* in order to receive His promised deliverance (salvation from the hand of the wicked). All men know this standard since it is God's creation, that can't be avoided, that declares His righteousness and right to judge.[2] So much is this the case that it should not surprise anyone that God predicts *universal salvation* with *universal service* by all the nations of the earth one day:

---

[1] This is one reason for believing that entrance into the Messianic Kingdom promised to David's descendant is not a grace issue. It must be a works issue. Without following the way in which one is instructed by God, he will not inherit/enter the kingdom. Jesus' interaction with the rich young ruler explicitly tells us that inheriting the kingdom is the same thing as entering the kingdom and both of these are the same are being saved.
[2] Ps. 50:6. Cf., Ps. 19:1-6; 97:1-9.

"So *the nations* will fear the name of the Lord, and *all the kings of the earth* Thy glory, for the Lord has built up Zion; He has appeared in His glory . . . that men may tell of the name of the Lord in Zion, and His praise in Jerusalem; when *the peoples* are gathered together, and *the kingdoms*, to *serve* the Lord." (Ps. 102:15, 22, emphases mine)

The time frame described here is sometime in the future. Paul and Luke describe it as the result of the Messiah's final military victory over His enemies and over the hand of all who hate Israel.[1] This deliverance is offered to all the nations. If a person, wherever he may live, *fears God and does what is right*, he will be included in the great salvation in the future. That salvation is the returning Messiah-King removing all wickedness from the earth and beginning His rule over all the earth as has been promised both in the OT and in the NT. But faith (fearing God) and good works (ordering your life aright) are needed for this salvation.

Do not make the mistake of assuming that faith in God requires faith in Jesus. That is not the case. If it were the case, then there could be no universal will of God at all because not everyone has had the opportunity to hear the message about Jesus.

King Solomon's Conclusion about Life

The Book of Ecclesiastes is basically a record of King Solomon's search for meaning and purpose in life, accompanied with the experience of happiness and fulfillment. His conclusion was that if man took life and what it had to offer on its own terms by itself, then life is all vanity. Everything in life and everything about life is vanity. Solomon pursued wisdom, pleasure, wealth, working hard (labor), oppression, rest, honor, and all else that

---

[1] Rom. 11:25-27; Lk. 1:70-71, respectively.

offered even the suggestion that it might give meaning and purpose along with happiness and fulfillment. Nothing could fulfill its own promises to give those things. Man must find these things somewhere else. Solomon concluded that man must find them in a relationship with God.

Solomon discovered that life was never meant to be lived in isolation from God. It was meant to be lived in fellowship with Him. Living life correctly requires a spiritual element that brings meaning and purpose, happiness and fulfillment, and complete contentment together. Solomon gave a summary on all of his research into the meaning of life when he said,

> "The conclusion, when all has been heard, is: *fear God and keep His commandments*, because this applies to *every person*. For God will bring *every act to judgment*, everything which is hidden, whether it be good or evil." (Eccl. 12:13-14, emphases mine)

Observe that Solomon, the wisest person who ever lived, listed the same two things that we have seen since Job first gave them in Job 1:8: *fear God and do what is right* (which is always to obey God, keeping His commandments). Should anyone ignore the conclusion of the wisest man who ever lived? Could God's requirements be simpler than Solomon has outlined?

Notice that this is advice that can be given to *every person* regardless of where he lives. So, meaning, purpose, happiness, and fulfillment can be attained by every person throughout the world if he only does these two things, *fear God and obey whatever instructions he has from God*. When we get to the NT, we will find these instructions spelled out again in the same general terms. *God's universal will does not change between the testaments.* Even when Jesus comes upon the scene in the beginning of the NT, the universal will of God for all men is not altered or replaced.

Finally, notice that the commands that will bring fulfillment in life, if heeded, will not keep one from this final judgment; it will cover every thought, feeling, and action that a person has given his whole life long. Solomon is clear that both good actions and evil actions will be judged. The outcome of this judgment will determine what a person experiences in the afterlife. This judgment cannot be avoided by belief in Jesus because it is for every person regardless of what or in whom he has believed.

This isn't simply an OT doctrine to be held until Jesus arrived on the scene and died on the cross. Paul warned everyone of exactly the same thing twenty-five years after Jesus died:

> "For *we* must *all* appear before *the judgment seat of Christ,* that *each one* may be *recompensed* (or paid back) for his *deeds* in the body, according to *what he has done,* whether *good or bad.*" (2Cor. 5:10, emphases and parenthesis mine)

Christ's work on the cross does not alleviate this judgment in the slightest. Whatever a person has done will be judged by God in all righteousness and given a just recompense. *What Jesus paid for on the cross in full* were the consequences of our sins that would separate us from God and hinder our fellowship with Him in this life. *There are no payments for personal stewardships, delegated by God, which were badly handled in this life.* Nevertheless, all stewardships will be justified by God if they had been executed with a fear of Him and an obedience to the instructions He gave pertaining to those stewardships.

How much Solomon knew about a coming Messiah's death for sin is unknown. That can't be said of Paul, however. Both Solomon and Paul agree on the coming judgment. They also agree that the judgment will be on everything that a person has done, both the good and the evil or wicked. But neither offers the least bit of hope that either faith in God or faith in Jesus frees a person from any negative consequences at that judgment. This point is taken beyond debate by Paul's personal testimonies recorded in the book of Acts. Having been instructed by Jesus personally for at least three years, which instruction must have included the accomplishments of Christ's own death, he still believed in his own coming judgment for everything he had done.[1] We ought to do the same.

Micah Explained What God Requires

Passages like Micah 6:8 are so straightforward that few can miss their point. While the verse is addressed to Israel who was in rebellion toward God, the passage can be applied to all mankind. So, for example, I found it incredibly interesting that God warned *all the nations* that were coming against Israel in the last days that He was going to pour out His anger and wrath upon them because, now note this well, they had not *obeyed* Him.[2]

The Septuagint used the verb *to hear* or *to listen to someone* to translate the Hebrew term which refers to a *hearing* that gives attention to or has an interest in the one speaking. This hearing requires one to *listen to* Him, that is, to respond to Him in obedience.[3] It is similar to what parents mean when they say to their children, "Did you hear me?" When they say that, they are asking their children why aren't they obeying them. The same thing is meant by God when He wants *all men to hear Him*.

God's judgment will come upon those who are trying to destroy Israel in the last days. His judgment will be deserved

---

[1] Gal. 1:10-18; Acts 24:14-16, 24-25; 2Cor. 5:10.
[2] Mic. 5:15.
[3] Francis Brown, S.R. Driver, and Charles A. Briggs, A Hebrew and English Lexicon of the Old Testament. Oxford, Clarendon Press, 1972, p. 1033. The same term is used in Micah 3:9 as well.

because those nations will not have listened to Him as He communicated with them in His typically clear way. Even when God's judgment begins to fall upon them in those last days, if they repent of their sins,[1] He will forgive their sins, as He has done at other times,[2] and redirect His wrath and anger upon others.[3]

What does God want Israel and all other persons around the world to do in order to avoid His judgments upon them? Micah asked that question and then answered it when he said:

> "He has told you, O man, what is good, and what does the Lord require of you but to *do justice*, to *love kindness*, and to *walk humbly* with your God?" (Mic. 6:8)

This is the same basic requirement that we have seen from the time of Job onward: *fear God and do what is right* (or obey Him). Walking humbly with God involves fearing Him, and doing justice and loving kindness covers the requirement of doing what is right. This is what God requires of all men to be *acceptable to Him*. God has made it simple for a reason: He wants all men to walk with Him and experience the blessings He desires to give.

God's OT Requirements Summarized in the NT

I'm dropping Heb. 11:6 into our discussion here because it is a summary of the requirements that God had for all the people in the OT if they wanted to live a life approved by God.[4] It is an amazingly simple and straightforward verse. It is also a verse that doesn't quite fit into Christianity's orthodox paradigm. The reason that it doesn't fit is that it doesn't require a person to have

---

[1] Rev. 9:20-21.
[2] Mk. 1:4; Acts 2:38-39.
[3] Cf., Rom. 1:18.
[4] Heb. 11:1-2.

faith in a coming Messiah in order to be approved by God. Orthodox Christianity cannot accept the idea that God can accept a person who had not believed in a coming Messiah in the OT or in Jesus in the NT.

I admit that this is one of my favorite verses, one that I have used throughout my ministry. But I must admit also that I only used the first part of the verse until about twelve years ago. I had used the verse only to emphasize the need for faith in the walk of a Christian. But now I have come to see the great importance of the second half of the verse for all people of every era. The whole verse says,

> "And without *faith* it is impossible to please (*Him*), for he who comes to God must *believe that* He is, *and that* He is a rewarder of those who seek Him." (Heb. 11:6, emphases and parenthesis mine)

While the first part of the verse requires a faith response from a person who wants to please God, the last part of the verse gives the content of that faith, generally speaking. The one who comes to God must believe two things: that He exists, and that He is a rewarder of those who seek Him. In this context, those who seek God are those who are responding to God's revelation of His will to them. Their faith is simply *their response of agreement* to what God is asking them to consider or to perform.

This is exactly what faith is in all periods of human history. *Faith is man's hearing or reception or positive response to God who is revealing His will.* When God speaks, He only requires man to "listen," that is, to be receptive to what He is saying to him and follow it. The fact that God continues to speak to all men in various ways requires a commensurate ability within all men to hear and to respond to God's communications. Otherwise, His overtures in communicating with man would be futile, even senseless. Surely

God knows that this would be the case if man were unable to respond to His communications! Are we grasping the significance of this fact?

There are seventeen different examples given by the author of the book of Hebrews of individuals responding to God. Some people are used more than once. These examples cover those who responded to His revelation to them *before* the Law was given[1] and those who responded to Him *after* the Law had been given.[2]

These seventeen examples accomplish two purposes. First, they illustrate the nature of faith described in verse one of this chapter. Ultimately the essence of faith will be the same in every other use of the term when referring to personal faith throughout the Bible. There is no other kind of faith than this kind. Second, the seventeen examples of faith show how men found approval with God in the OT, demonstrating the meaning of Heb. 11:2. There is no approval if there is no faith being exercised, regardless of the obedience that might be offered. Obedience without faith is a moral response toward men and thus beneficial to all.

What are the two things that constitute the content of faith? One, that there is a God who is speaking to you. Two, that this God will reward anyone who seeks Him by responding to His revelations to him. In other words, if you seek Him, you will find Him. If you trust in His word to you, He will bless you for it.

All this is so simple, so straightforward. Fear God. That is, know that He is exists and that He has the authority to judge. Obey Him. On the positive side, understand that your obedience will bring about a response from God. He loves to reward or bless those who keep His instructions.

---

[1] Heb. 11:4-29.
[2] Heb. 11:30-40.

This verse presents a simple overview of how to live a life that God can justify. To believe in God's existence and in His desire to reward those who seek Him is clearly set before us in the examples of chapter eleven of Hebrews as *fearing God and obeying Him.* These are the two conditions that people had to fulfill to be acceptable to God in the OT. Did these conditions change when Jesus finally came upon the scene?

Jesus Gave us the Same Two Requirements

When we enter the NT, we find that nothing has changed; God's standard for a person to be *acceptable* to Him is still expressed in *fearing God* (or some fruit of that fear) *and doing what is right.* Whether Jesus had in mind Solomon's conclusion on life or not, He reiterated the basic elements of that conclusion in His teachings. He affirmed that all of the thirty-nine books of revelation given to the Jewish people explained how they were to conduct their lives. All of the thirty-nine books of revelation could be fulfilled if they loved God and loved their neighbors as they loved themselves.[1]

That is an astounding statement! How simple. Jesus summarized God's requirements for the Jewish people into loving God and loving one's neighbor. If we used the prophet Micah's wording, we would say, "This, O man, is what the Lord requires." And God requires it from both the Jewish people and the Gentiles alike.[2] They both were *to love God and to love their neighbor as they loved themselves.* God really intended life to be this simple.

It is basic to understand that the OT was given to the Jewish people to guide them in living life in a way that was *acceptable* to

---

[1] Matt. 22:34-40.
[2] Lk. 10:25-37; 1John 2:15-17; 3:16-18.

God.[1] Consequently, if Jesus can summarize that information into two commands for the Jewish people,[2] and if we already have evidence from the OT that the same standard applied to *every man in every nation* under the sun,[3] we can rightly conclude that *if any man feared God and did what was right,[4] that man was fully acceptable to God even though he may not have believed in Jesus.*

While it may be shocking to realize the following fact, it nevertheless is true that believing in Jesus (or for the people in the OT, believing in the coming Messiah) has never been a condition for a person to be acceptable to God and in right relationship with Him. It should not escape our attention that, when *Jesus* summarized the OT requirements into two commands, He did not include believing in Himself or in a coming Messiah as part of the requirements to be *acceptable* to God. Surely He would know what was needed to be acceptable to the Father! We will have further proof as we continue through the NT that Jesus only required these two conditions for a man to be pleasing to God.

A Lawyer Understood God's Will Correctly

When Jesus interacted with the rich young ruler and, on another occasion, a lawyer, the question was raised, "What must I do to *inherit* (or to *have* or to *obtain*) eternal life?"[5] Now if you were asked that question, and you couldn't turn to a passage in the Bible before answering it, how would you answer it? What does a person need to do to inherit or to have or to obtain eternal life? Most would answer it according to the predominate mindset

---

[1] E.g., Ps. 119.

[2] Cf., Lk. 11:42, here stated as justice and love for God.

[3] Job 1:8; Gen. 20:1-11; Eccl. 12:13-14.

[4] Cf., the parable of Lk. 18:1-8.

[5] Mk. 10:16-17, 23-24; Lk. 18:18 and Lk. 10:25. These verbs are used interchangeably.

within Christendom today. They would say, "A person obtains/inherits eternal life by believing in Jesus." Yet on the two occasions listed here, *Jesus* was asked that question, and *He* did not require the person to have faith in Him for the obtainment of eternal life.

In both of these cases, that of the lawyer and that of the rich young ruler, Jesus pointed to the OT to obtain the proper answer to the question. That is a very important observation. *Whatever eternal life referred to in these two instances, the means of obtaining it could be gleaned from a study of the OT Scriptures.* However, the eternal life that Jesus was giving to those who believed in Him cannot be found in the OT at all unless, of course, we insistently read it into the OT in order to then find it there.

The spiritual life that Jesus was giving, which was also called eternal life, cannot be found in the OT. It was first given by Jesus when a person placed faith in Him as Messiah during His earthly ministry. It was never given to anyone in the OT. One reason for that is it was never offered there. Another reason is that no one could have believed in *Jesus* since He was not known by that name in the OT. Remember it is *His own life* that is being offered.

The eternal life that the two passages under consideration refer to is not the *spiritual life* that can be possessed and experienced by believing in Jesus today. It refers to *the life* that is coming in *the age to come*. Both the lawyer and the rich young ruler were asking how they could *enter* the kingdom of Messiah when it comes.[1] Jesus clearly explained that the *entrance into His future kingdom is based upon works* just like we saw in the OT. Entrance into the kingdom is not a grace issue. Consequently, grace alone through faith alone will not obtain entrance into this kingdom. Jesus made this

---

[1] Matt. 19:23-24; Lk. 10:25-28.

as clear as anyone could make it.

In the lawyer's case, Jesus began answering his question by asking a question: "What is written in the Law?" In other words, the answer that you are looking for, sir, is given to you in the Law of Moses. That Law was given as a guide for living, not as a means for being *saved* (in the sense taught by orthodox, Christian theology); the Law was never given as a means of getting a person to heaven. But it was given as a means for entering the Kingdom of Heaven which is the Messiah's earthly kingdom. The Law explained the righteousness that God required for entering the Messiah's kingdom as living life the right way. Without this lifestyle of righteousness, or right living, entrance into the coming kingdom would be impossible. Just as King David had done in Psalm 25:12-13, Jesus did here: He made the entrance into the kingdom a works issue.

When the lawyer answered his own question from the Law, and then summarized the OT, just like Jesus had done in Matt. 22:34-40, he affirmed that if a person loved God and loved his neighbor as himself, he would make it into the Kingdom of Messiah. Such an answer, if given today, would make most of Christianity's orthodox teachers bristle with rejection. "Where is belief in Jesus?" they would ask. Where is the gospel of grace alone through faith alone? No one gets into the kingdom without believing in Jesus. Right? Wrong!

Jesus, the King of the coming kingdom and the one who had been offering the kingdom to Israel throughout His ministry, responded clearly and directly to the lawyer's answer, saying,

> *"You have answered correctly!* Do this (the two commands of loving God and loving your neighbor), and you will live (in the age called eternal life, inheriting or entering that age by these works)." (Lk. 10:28, emphasis and parentheses mine)

Jesus had basically outlined the same path for the rich young ruler when He answered how he could inherit or obtain *an eternal life to come* (not the eternal life that is available to a person when he trusts in Jesus either initially or subsequently), a *life* in a future kingdom. This future *life* was what he was seeking.[1] And it is the life that we should be offering to the whole world today.

The extraordinary surprise in Jesus' answers to the rich young ruler and to the lawyer is two-fold. First, there is no requirement to believe in Jesus to be *saved* in order to enter the Kingdom of Messiah. The *salvation* that Jesus brings upon His return to earth is a physical rescue for those who are fighting for their lives, but who are living righteously at the same time.[2] That salvation has nothing to do with going to heaven. It doesn't necessarily even require a belief in Jesus.[3] Both the OT and the NT require practical righteousness, done in faith, to enter the kingdom of heaven.

Second, Jesus agreed with the lawyer's conclusion concerning the commands that were binding on each individual who wanted to enter the Kingdom of Messiah. These two commandments had to be obeyed for anyone to obtain or inherit *eternal life* which, in these two instances, is synonymous to the *Kingdom of Messiah*. There is no natural way of turning Jesus' conditions for entrance into the kingdom into a grace alone standard. Loving God and loving one's neighbor were required for entrance. Love cannot be performed apart from deeds.[4]

---

[1] Mk. 10:17-30. Note carefully that in Mk. 10:30 *the age to come* is the time and place where eternal life is obtained. Notice also that *inheriting* the kingdom is described as *entering* the kingdom by Jesus (Mk. 10:17. 24-25) and *entering* into that future kingdom is referred to by Peter, with Jesus in agreement, as being *save* (Mk. 10:26). Since these terms are used interchangeably here, they must not be differentiated due to one's theological beliefs.
[2] Heb. 9:27-28.
[3] Matt. 25:31-46. These Gentiles enter the kingdom due to their good deeds alone.
[4] Cf., John 14:21; 1John 3:17-18.

This does not need to be confusing. If someone asks you, "What must a person do to enter or inherit the kingdom of Messiah (that is, to be saved into the age to come)?" you should answer just as Jesus did: love God and love your neighbor as yourself. But if someone asks you, "What must a person do to experience eternal life now (that is, how do I receive the abundant life that Jesus offers)?" you should answer just as Jesus explained: believe in Me, and you shall have eternal life.[1]

There is more than one referent for eternal life and for being saved. Don't let someone confuse inheriting eternal life in the future with experiencing eternal life now. The Biblical references to the phrase *eternal life* can refer to one of two things: the supernatural, abundant life that Jesus gives a person whenever he trusts Jesus[2] for it or to the age to come.[3] In exactly the same way, *salvation* can refer to two different things. First, it can refer to the deliverance or rescue a person experiences from the bondage of his trespasses and sins.[4] This salvation is accomplished by the use of the gift of eternal life each time a person trusts in Jesus[5] for the resources needed to overcome his sins. Second, it can also refer to the coming age of Messiah.[6] But neither *eternal life* nor *salvation* ever refers to (going to) heaven or (escaping from) hell.

Jesus' agreement with the lawyer's conclusion reiterates the simple, two-fold requirement that needs to be fulfilled in order for a person to be *acceptable* to God. What is remarkable is the fact that the lawyer answered Jesus' question in exactly the same way that Jesus had answered the Pharisees' question earlier in His

---

[1] John 6:47.
[2] E.g., John 4:10-14; 6:47.
[3] E.g., Dan. 12:2. Cf., Mk. 10:30; Lk. 10:25-28.
[4] Matt. 1:21. We should understand Eph. 2:1-9 in terms of Matt. 1:21.
[5] E.g., Eph. 2:4, 8-9.
[6] E.g., Rom. 1:16; 11:25-27.

ministry. Jesus authoritatively affirmed in both instances the continuity of the standard for acceptance with God in both ages, the past age of the OT saint and the present age of the church. If a person loves God and loves his neighbor as he loves himself, he will be acceptable to God and qualified to enter the Messiah's kingdom whenever it is established. *We must accept the fact that God's universal standard that we have seen repeated in the OT has continued on into the NT and beyond.* Through this lens we are meant to evaluate all men wherever they may live.

If loving God and others is the standard for being acceptable to God in general and for entrance into the coming earthly Kingdom of Messiah in specific, then we obviously need to make some adjustments in our thinking. Without a doubt works are involved in entering that Kingdom;[1] entering the kingdom and inheriting the kingdom refer to the same thing according to Jesus;[2] and loving properly always involves good deeds.[3]

But most importantly, when Jesus agreed with the Lawyer's assessment about the conditions needed for inheriting the kingdom of heaven, He showed that He continued to uphold the two conditions for being acceptable to God, namely, loving God and loving others. And when we let the Bible tell us what love is and what it does, we discover that loving God involves obeying Him[4] because we rightly fear Him.[5] We also discover that loving others is simply doing what is right toward them.[6] In short, *Jesus confirmed the continuation of the universal will of God for all men.*

---

[1] Matt. 5:20; 7:21.
[2] Matt. 19:16-17, 24-25.
[3] 1John 3:16-18.
[4] Deut. 6:4-9; 10:12-14; John 14:21
[5] Ex. 20:18-20; Heb. 10:31.
[6] Rom. 12:9-21; 13:7-8.

The Man Born Blind

The healing of the man who had been born blind is given in some detail in the Gospel of John, chapter nine. After the man's healing, the religious leaders began to argue with him. In the process of this argument, these religious leaders tried to intimidate him into agreeing with them that since Jesus did this healing on the Sabbath, He must be a sinner (a Law-breaker).[1] The blind man's response has become a classic answer used by all Christians who are being tempted to malign Jesus in some way. He said to the religious leaders,

> "Whether He is a sinner, I do not know; one thing I do know, that, whereas I was blind, now I see." (John 9:25)

It is very difficult to argue with someone else's personal experience. He has had an experience; that cannot be debated. Whether his experience is according to the truth that God has revealed to us is another matter, however. This man's experience denied the conclusions that the religious leaders wanted to draw about Jesus. His experience seemed, rather, to agree with the teachings that he had heard from childhood, teachings which the religious leaders themselves must have taught him. Consequently, his convicting response to them was using the truth that he had probably learned from them:

> "*We* know that God does not hear sinners; but if anyone is *God-fearing*, and *does His will*, He hears him." (John 9:31)

Boom! This man blew the bigoted religious leaders' arguments up. In his short but powerful statement, he made three points. First, the blind man argued from the common ground he had with the religious leaders. They both believed that God does not hear

---

[1] John 9:24.

sinners. Yet they were condemning Jesus as a sinner because He healed on the Sabbath even though it was obvious that God had heard His prayer for the man's healing.

Second, the blind man referred to the same two qualifications that we have seen repeated throughout the Bible up to this point. *Fearing God and doing what is right* (here what is right is identified as *God's will*), *makes one acceptable to God.* The blind man was affirming these characteristics about Jesus and in doing so he not only was giving the reason for his healing but establishing the fact that Jesus must be acceptable to God.

Think about that for a moment. Has that fact really been weighed truthfully in your convictions? It is true as it stands without any theological adjustments needing to be made upon it. Is a Mormon, for example, or a Hindu, or a Muslim acceptable to God because he fears God and does what is right? Is he acceptable to God without the necessity of believing in Jesus? That is what is being said here as it has been said from the book of Job throughout the OT.

The third point is simply the conclusion of the second point. *Wherever a person might live and whatever a person's religious culture might be, if he fears God and performs the instructions revealed to him by God, he can be assured that his prayers will be answered by God.* Not only were the apostle John, who wrote this narrative, and Jesus, who knew the thoughts and convictions of the blind man's heart and who probably discussed those convictions with John after this episode was over, on the same page with the blind man, they gave us no reason to doubt the premise the blind man used to answer the religious leaders. Since it is the same premise given repeatedly throughout the Bible, there is no reason to deny its validity here. Nor is there any reason to add to it the necessity of believing in Jesus. *A person can be acceptable to God without believing in Jesus.* But he must love/fear God and do what is right. This was what the blind man had been taught and, more importantly, what Jesus modeled before him, continuing to affirm God's universal will for all men.

Peter Finally Understands it

Luke's statement in Acts 10:34-35 is a profoundly important one since it comes some years after the death, resurrection, and ascension of Jesus. One of the standard ways to sidestep any Biblical teaching that does not fit the theological system that a person might adhere to is to restrict it to an earlier age in the Bible. Since many of the verses used to identify God's universal will for all men are from the OT, some may suggest that God's will has changed now that Jesus had come and died for the sins of the world. Many things did, of course, change. But the performance of the universal will of God in order to be accepted by God was not one of those things.

All the passages used from the NT actually are proofs that such a change has not taken place. This last, simple citation of the two requirements by God for a person to be *acceptable* to Him is not only given by Peter, one of Jesus' apostles who constitute part of the foundation of the church,[1] but it is also declared to be true of Cornelius, a Gentile, *before* he ever heard Peter's message about Jesus and became *saved* (at least in the minds of many). *Being acceptable to God in this life and prepared to meet Him in the afterlife is not the same thing as being saved* according to the Scriptures. In fact Cornelius is never described in this episode as a saved person.

---

[1] Eph. 2:20.

56

This passage has caused a great deal of spiritual heartburn in the lives of many pastors. The reason for this is quite obvious. This passage gives us information that does not support orthodox Christian theology. The interpretive method of Cinderella's slipper must be used in order to make it fit.

How can a person need to be *justified* (in the orthodox Christian sense) in order to, *supposedly*, obtain the needed righteousness for a permanent standing before God if he is already *righteous* before God?

Why would a person need to believe in Jesus in order to be saved (again, used as orthodox Christian theology defines it as going to heaven when one dies) if he is already completely acceptable to God before he believes in Jesus?

This passage, then, exposes some of the errors of what has been preached in our churches and taught in our seminaries for the last five hundred years, if not longer. One of the major problems that this passage presents is its simplicity. It says,

> "And opening his mouth, Peter said: 'I most certainly understand [*now*] that God is not one to show partiality, but *in every nation* the man who *fears Him* and *does what is right* is *welcome* [or *acceptable*] to Him." (emphases and brackets mine)

There are three obvious truths here for everyone to see. First, this perspective is a new one for Peter. He had just recently come to this conclusion.[1] Before this he thought that the Gentiles did not have the same relationship with God that the Jews had. After all the Jews were God's chosen people and the Gentiles were not. God's thrice repeated vision of the sheet coming down out of heaven with unclean animals on it and the command to kill and

---

[1] The present tense describes Peter's present condition of awareness. He is presently comprehending matters that he had been wrong on before his vision of the sheets coming down out of heaven and his trip to Cornelius' home.

eat those animals prepared Peter to see Cornelius and his household as God saw them. *They were righteous and acceptable to God before they ever heard about Jesus.*

Second, Peter realizes that God could not have established any stricter standard than the two requirements He had laid down for all men. Think through this carefully. God could not have established any stricter requirements for all men throughout the whole world to fulfill than that of *fearing Him and doing what is right.* If He had, the apostle Peter says that He would not have been *impartial* in His judgment of the different people groups in their different cultures, growing up with their different religious convictions.

What the apostle Peter is saying is this: if God had required all men to believe in Jesus in order for them to go to heaven, *He would be showing partiality in His judgments* since most of the people who have ever lived have never had the information about Jesus so they could believe in Him. No one can believe in someone about whom they have never heard.

If Peter drew this conclusion, shouldn't we do the same? God remains impartial only if He requires all men to be responsible for information that they have actually been given. Whatever God requires for a person to be welcomed or acceptable to Him must be available to everyone who has ever lived, or God becomes an impartial, unfair judge.

Third, it is critical to understand Peter's declaration here. He says that *every person*, regardless of the country he comes from or the religion that he was taught, *who fears God and does what is right is acceptable (or welcomed) to Him.* These are the same two requirements that we have seen over and over again throughout the Scriptures. The obvious conundrum that orthodox Christianity faces is this: Peter has travelled to Cornelius' house in Caesarea in order to preach Jesus to him so that he could be *saved;*[1] but he is declaring that Cornelius was already *righteous*[2] and *acceptable*[3] to God *before* he ever heard about Jesus.

This leaves us to conclude that neither the *righteousness* that is supposedly needed for a person to go to heaven nor a person's *acceptability* before God is based upon believing in Jesus. Rather these things are based upon being the kind of person Cornelius already was.[4] Cornelius fulfilled *the universal will of God*, which he probably learned from his Jewish mentors, and was, therefore, acceptable to God before he ever heard of Jesus or had an opportunity to believe in Him for the *salvation* He offered.[5]

We must understand that Peter was clearly declaring a profound truth here: *God would be partial if He required the whole world to believe in Jesus in order to be acceptable to Him.* The reason is simple. Not everyone has had access to the good news about Jesus in order to believe it. Consequently, when we share our faith in Jesus with others, our purpose is not to make Christ's righteousness available to them (one error) or for them to receive a forgiveness of sins (a second error) that makes heaven obtainable (a third error). We share Jesus for reasons much higher than those.

The last several pages of OT and NT verses show us that God has given a very consistent message throughout the successive ages of human history. God requires all men to fulfill two basic

---

[1] Acts 11:14.

[2] Acts 10:1-4, 22, 35. He was a doer of righteousness (v. 35) because he was a righteous person (Acts 10:22 where "just" is equivalent to "righteous") who feared God (v. 22). And he was this before exercising faith in Jesus.

[3] Acts 10:35.

[4] Acts 10:1-4,22.

[5] Acts 11:14-18. This salvation is not the same as that mentioned in Eph. 2:8-9 because Cornelius was not dead in his trespasses and sins as the Ephesians were. This salvation is the future deliverance of Messiah into His kingdom (Acts 15:1-11; 16:14-34).

requirements to be acceptable to Him. They need to love God and to love their neighbors as they love themselves. There are many other truths to learn because the more a person knows the wiser he will be in living a spiritually productive life in a world turned away from God.

On the other hand, if there is anything in our lives that we are either addicted to or that we habitually perform that is contrary to either of these two simple requirements, we need to ask God for Jesus' life to overcome them as quickly and as consistently as possible. If fulfilling the two requirements makes one acceptable with God, then failing to fulfill these two requirements brings God's displeasure in this age and a negative judgment at the Judgment Seat of Christ.

No one will have the sins that he is committing now overlooked or graciously dismissed at the Judgment Seat of Christ. Jesus did not die so that a person can live an irresponsible life. The forgiveness that He offers enables a person to come back into fellowship with God during his earthly life.[1] But Jesus does not offer a forgiveness that can be applied at His Judgment Seat. That is the only straightforward way there is to understand either Solomon's conclusion on life[2] or the apostle Paul's warning to Christians about the coming judgment.[3] Every deed will be evaluated and a recompense attached to it. That recompense must be paid before a person can move forward with his life.[4]

This is a judgment that only God is able to pronounce. It will not be black and white as we might see it. He will have information that we don't have and use wisdom that is beyond our

---

[1] 1John 1:3—2:3-6.
[2] Eccl. 12:13-14.
[3] 2Cor. 5:10; Rom. 14:10-12. Cf., also Acts 24:14-16.
[4] Cf., Matt. 18:34-35.

grasp. It won't be a matter of justice alone. Grace, mercy, and for-giveness (but not one required by the death of Christ alone) will also be involved. I can't even imagine how vastly different His judgment will be since His wisdom is so far above that of all humans combined. If we are supposed to fear God's judgment during our earthly lives, there is, obviously, reasons to fear it in the afterlife. Nevertheless, this judgment will come from a Father who loves each person with an infinite love, longing to dos what is necessary so that He can have the most intimate relationship with each person He has created.

Chapter 3

The Need to be Better at Knowing the God of Love

God is not looking for people to judge. Yet that seems to be the thrust of a great many messages that are preached today. It may be that I believe this because of the limited and narrow daily experience I have with certain denominations that focus more heavily upon God's wrath and judgment than others do. If that be the case, I thank God for the others who bring a balance to the Biblical message.

I remember in my very early days of ministry that I was introduced to a book on the nature of God, written by Stephen Charnock and entitled *The Existence and Attributes of God*. I remember how impressed I was, and still am, with his meditations on the Scriptures as he expounded God's nature. In that book the author makes a case for the holiness of God being central to and foundational for all the other attributes of God. He used Isa. 6:3 to argue for his proposition, saying that there is no other attribute thrice invoked as God's holiness is here. With that observation he began to draw the conclusion that God's holiness must be the key to understanding all the other attributes of God.

That is an impressive observation. But as I grew in my own facility to interpret the Word of God, I began to question some of the things that I had been taught, especially if they were *deductions* by men trying to give an accurate picture of the teachings of the Bible. Now after over forty-eight years of ministry experience,

63

I have returned to the Biblical emphasis that I had learned early in my ministry training before I had the privilege of attending seminary for academic instruction. Yes, seminary training is a privilege, but it must be undertaken warily. I now realize that it is God's love that the Bible places central to everything that He is, or at least to everything that He wishes me to focus upon, as a foundation for my thinking and ministry.

When I take the Bible seriously for what it says, I am forced to conclude that when the Bible says that God loves the whole world, then He must love the whole world. Regardless of the forced interpretations that are offered to deny this truth or to limit the scope of this truth, the Bible is too clear on this subject to allow for even the slightest bit of hesitation about accepting this proposition as true. So, for example, the Bible says:

> "For God so loved *the world* that He gave His only begotten Son that whoever believes in Him should not perish, but have eternal life." (John 3:16)

> "... 'Behold, the Lamb of God who takes away the sin of *the world*.'" (John 1:29)

> "For God did not send His Son into the world to judge *the world*, but that *the world* should be saved through Him." (John 3:17)

> "and they were saying to the woman, 'It is no longer because of what you said that we believe, for we have heard for ourselves and know that this One is indeed the Savior of *the world*, the Christ." (John 4:42 in the Hodges and Farstad Greek Text)

> "For the bread of God is that which comes down out of heaven and gives life to *the world*." (John 6:33)

> "I am the living bread that came down out of heaven; if anyone eats of this bread, he shall live forever; and the bread also which I shall give *for the life of the world* is My flesh." (John 6:51)

"...'I am the light of *the world*; he who follows Me shall not walk in the darkness, but shall have the light of life." (John 8:12)

"And I, if I be lifted up from the earth, will draw *all men* to Myself." (John 12:32)

"And if anyone hears My sayings, and does not keep them, I do not judge him; for I did not come to *judge the world*, but to *save the world*." (John 12:47)

"And He [the Holy Spirit], when He comes, will convict *the world* concerning sin, and righteousness, and judgment." (John 16:8)

How many times does God have to say something, and how many ways must He use to say it, before we finally receive His revelation as true? God loves the whole world. If we want to be sons of God, we must do the same thing.[1] God has set the standard, and if we are going to be like Him, *if we are going to be* a *son*, we must carry out the standard that He has set.

I'm sure that you noticed that all of the passages used above are from only one book of the NT. So many more passages could be marshaled if the need were present. The one book that I used above is the one that is traditionally identified as the *evangelistic gospel*, the book that challenges us to take the message of Jesus to the entire world. When the Spirit came after Jesus' ascension, everyone who believed in Jesus as Messiah was given the task of being a witness to the rest of the world even if those in the world reject or respond in anger toward that message.[2]

God is a God of love. We should notice His own emphasis concerning His nature when He revealed Himself to Moses after judging the people for their sin with the golden calf:

---

[1] Matt. 5:43-48. Notice that being a son of God is *a conditional status*. That is a fact that must be incorporated into our thinking as we continue to investigate orthodox Christianity and the ramifications of this new paradigm.

[2] John 15:26—16:11; 17:18; Acts 1:8; Lk. 24:47; etc.

"The Lord, the Lord God, *compassionate and gracious*, slow to anger, and *abounding in lovingkindness* and truth; *who keeps lovingkindness for thousands*, who forgives iniquity, transgression and sin; yet He will by no means leave the guilty unpunished, visiting the iniquity of fathers upon the children and on the grandchildren to the third and fourth generations." (Ex. 34:6-7).

God's compassion and lovingkindness dominate the description that God gave of Himself.[1] What we find here in God's self-disclosure is exactly what we see in Jesus who came to represent the Father in all things.[2] He had compassion for the depressed and downcast[3] just as He did for the struggling disciple.[4] He loved His own apostles to the very end of His life,[5] inviting them to continue to abide in His love after He was gone.[6]

Our God is a God of love. There is never a cessation of the flow of His love toward us.[7] But while no trial or affliction can separate us from the experience of God's love,[8] nevertheless, we may choose not to abide in it for myriad reasons. One of the world's greatest needs is to be loved for who each one is, and God is ready to do that.[9] Walking in that love will not only get a person through this life, but it will prepare him for the afterlife as well.[10]

---

[1] Furthermore, the apostle Paul explained for us that forgiveness is a characteristic of love (1Cor. 13:4-8a).

[2] E.g., Heb. 1:3; John 14:7-9; Matt. 9:36.

[3] Matt. 9:36.

[4] Mk. 10:22.

[5] John 13:1.

[6] John 15:9-10.

[7] Rom. 8:38-39.

[8] Rom. 8:35-37.

[9] 1John 4:7-16.

[10] 1John 4:16-18.

Chapter 4

The Need to be Better at
Pursuing Kingdom Entrance *As a Believer*

There is probably no more basic distinction to make in one's approach to Bible study than understanding the difference between being saved (regardless of the view you hold on salvation) and entering the Kingdom of Heaven (or the Kingdom of God, its complete equivalent). In Jesus' presentation of the gospel that He preached,[1] *the gospel of the Kingdom*,[2] which is far removed from *the gospel of grace* touted by orthodox Christianity today, He addressed His apostles and a multitude along with them. Apparently, the truths about the Kingdom that Jesus set forth were as applicable to one group as they were to the other group. He certainly made no distinction between the two groups during His discourse. Consequently, it was irrelevant whether a person had been saved or not since both the saved (represented by the apostles, we have *assumed*) and the unsaved (represented by the multitudes, we have *assumed*) were all being invited to enter the Kingdom on the same bases.[3]

I know that for many readers that last paragraph may be a bit confusing because of the teachings that they have been exposed to for so long. People talk about believing in Jesus and entering the kingdom as though they were the same thing. But they aren't. We also talk about being saved and entering the kingdom as

---

[1] Matt. 5:1—7:29.
[2] Matt. 4:23; 9:35; 24:13-14.
[3] Matt. 5:20; 6:33; 7:21.

though they were the same thing. But they aren't either. We've heard about a *gospel of grace*, which is supposed to offer forgiveness of sins, a righteous standing before God, and a guaranteed eternal destiny in heaven. And the wonderful thing about this gospel is that it doesn't require any works for obtaining these three marvelous gifts.

But when the Bible, and not man's theological constructions of the Bible, is one's plumb line for truth, then many become unsettled about whether the gospel is an offer of forgiveness and a guarantee of heaven. The reason for this unsettled state? There are just too many verses and concepts that can't be harmonized with a gospel offering these things unconditionally. There isn't just a tiny hold in the dam; the dam is cracked from bottom to top. The only reason it has held together for as long as it has may be contributed to the power and purposes of God.

But most importantly, there is no verse that *explicitly* states the universally *assumed* supposition that God is offering *through faith in Jesus* a forgiveness of sins that will guarantee an eternity with Him in the afterlife. *That gospel* is of man's own making. At the tower of Babel man tried to construct a means to reach heaven. Unfortunately, he is still trying to do so.

But *that gospel* is all we have ever heard preached. As a result, one would think it must be found everywhere in the Bible, especially in the NT. When I ask my friends for those verses, they look at me quite sheepishly and offer one of the classic verses, like John 3:16, for their answer. But when I point out the obvious fact that the verse they gave me does not *explicitly* say what we are looking for, they don't know where to go next.

Connected to the ideas of forgiveness and a guaranteed destiny is a corollary that we have also heard a million times: that

Jesus is our King, and that He is ruling over us today. He is our King, supposedly, because we have trusted in Him for eternal life, forgiveness, and that wonderfully attractive safe haven in heaven with God. But there are no Scripture passages that *explicitly* say any of these things.

In fact, the Bible very clearly says that Jesus is *not ruling today!* Rather than ruling on *His* throne, He is sitting beside the Father who is ruling on His own (the Father's) throne. And the Father will continue to rule until all of Jesus' enemies become a footstool for His feet.[1] Then Jesus will return to earth in order to ascend His glorious throne[2] and rule for a millennium.[3] So, rather than ruling over the world, the church, or us as individuals today, He is praying for us as our High Priest.[4]

Furthermore, *the Bible never invites a person to believe in Jesus to obtain forgiveness for all of his sins.* Jesus Himself even taught that there were other means of receiving forgiveness of sins[5] besides believing in Him. John the Baptist offered still another way to receive forgiveness.[6] These are clear, simple statements in the Scriptures. But obtaining forgiveness of sins is never *explicitly* said to come from believing in Jesus nor is obtaining this one-time forgiveness ever declared to be a condition for going to heaven (in the sense that we *assume* today). Those are connections that men have made without Scriptural support.

It is also a fact, and a most distressing one at that, that the Bible never *explicitly* offers heaven as a reward, benefit, or blessing for believing in Jesus. A person can believe in Jesus, and even

---

[1] Ps. 110:1.
[2] Matt. 25:31.
[3] Rev. 20:4-6.
[4] Heb. 7:25.
[5] Matt. 6:12.
[6] Mk. 1:4.

be His servant, and still end up in a place designated for the chastisement of unfaithful and unwise servants of Jesus.[1] Whether this place and the place for those who were never His servants in any consistent way is the same, remains to be seen.

It follows from all of this that we aren't furthering the kingdom today for the very reason that there is no kingdom to further. There is no King Jesus reigning today. And we seem to forget that Jesus came to be king of the Jews.[2] The Gentiles get blessed only when the Jews obtain their covenants and promises from God through the return of their Messiah to set up their kingdom.[3]

But we can further the proclamation of Jesus. He is giving *life* now as a motivation for all to pursue His future kingdom[4] that will one day be established. This kingdom is successfully sought today in the sense of its future establishment by fulfilling God's universal will in faith. Jesus *explicitly* affirmed this fact in a discussion on being a good neighbor with a lawyer.[5]

Dr. N.T. Wright has recently suggested that the whole scenario of believing in Jesus *in order to go to heaven* was adapted by the church from Platonic ideas. He says,

> "Western culture has been so wedded to the platonic idea that God's purpose for humans is to leave this world and go to 'heaven' to be with him – as opposed to the biblical idea that God's purpose for humans is to reflect the praises of creation back to him and to reflect his image in the world, so that ultimately heaven and earth will be one . . . ."[6]

---

[1] Matt. 24:45-51; Lk. 12:41-48.
[2] Matt. 2:2. An issue covered extensively in volume five of this Series.
[3] Rom. 11:11-15 and following.
[4] Matt. 6:33.
[5] Lk. 10:25-28.
[6] N.T. Wright, *The Revolution Has Begun: Reconsidering the Meaning of Jesus' Crucifixion*, Loc 1775ff, iPad reader.

His point is that from the time when the incorporation of Platonic ideas into the Biblical message began, the message changed its focus from earth to heaven. *Consequently, Christians have become obsessed with going to heaven instead of being enthralled with walking with God now as they fulfill the responsibilities delegated to them.*

Whether the emphasis upon going to heaven can be attached to the incorporation of Platonic ideas into the Christian message, I don't know. But what I am absolutely sure of is this: *the Bible does not give us any reason to believe that the goal of this life is discovering the right path to heaven so that we can live with God forever.* This life is about being faithful stewards of the various responsibilities that God has given to each of us. This fact is clearly presented to us in God's original design for man on earth,[1] in Jesus' delineation of the two greatest commands,[2] and in the parables of the Talents and the Minas.[3]

Jesus' death on the cross does not pay the penalties attached to poor stewardships. This fact is also clearly revealed to us in those same parables as well as in the story of the rich man and Lazarus. The fact that there is a judgment according to a man's works[4] should establish this truth forever in our consciences. Even in amoral issues there will be an accountability according to Rom. 14:10-12.

When you stand before the judgment seat, you will give an account of your own actions.[5] You will not be able to use someone else, either Jesus (and His supposed payment[6] on the cross for you) or a person who had misled you during your earthly life, as a reason for avoiding the judgment that is rightfully due to you.

---

[1] Gen. 1:26, 28; Ps. 8:4-6
[2] Matt. 22:34-40.
[3] Matt. 25:14-30 and Lk. 19:11-27, respectively.
[4] Matt. 16:24-27; Rev. 22:12.
[5] Rom. 14:12.
[6] John 19:30.

Just as no one can advise God now,[1] no one will be able to gainsay His judgments at the Judgment Seat.

The Messianic Kingdom will basically be a time when the will of God has come to earth as Jesus, being personally present upon the earth, is ruling over all the affairs of men. No longer will anyone pray the disciple's prayer: "Thy Kingdom come, Thy will be done on earth as it is in heaven." Rather, all men will pray something like this: Lord, I thank You that Your Kingdom has come just as You taught us it would if we prayed for it.

In this Kingdom there will be no more wars or rumors of wars. Every nation will be at peace with every other nation.[2] Israel will no longer be looked down upon or despised by anyone.[3] Rather, the Israeli nation will be the head of all other nations,[4] being cherished openly by God as the apple of His eye.

Every government will be righteous in its governance.[5] In fact, there will be no wickedness anywhere throughout the whole world.[6] Though men will sin, they will not develop a system or organization of corruption that takes advantage of others. There will be no shady, unethical, manipulative defense lawyers trying to keep guilty people out of prison. Every case will be tried from an objective point of reference for a righteous judgment to be given as the end goal.

Every nation will worship God just as Jesus has made Him known to the world through His incarnation.[7]

The medical field will be similar to the governments ruling all

---

[1] Rom. 11:33-36.
[2] Isa. 2:4; Hos. 2:18; etc.
[3] Ezek. 28:24.
[4] Deut. 28:13-14; Dan. 7:27.
[5] Isa. 9:7; Isa. 2:2-3; Acts 3:19-23; etc.
[6] Matt. 13:41-43.
[7] Isa. 2:2-4.

the nations of the world. It will probably be radically different from what it is today since most sickness and disease will be cured and kept from destroying the physical lives of those living during the millennial reign of Christ. If the Messiah was supposed to be identified by the miracles of healing that He performed during His offer of the Kingdom,[1] it only makes sense that those miraculous healings will continue until there are no afflicted left. This would be similar to what must have been true in the city of Capernaum during Jesus' earthly ministry. Because of Jesus' miraculous healings that were centered in and around that city, some scholars suppose that few were left to be healed.

Even the animal kingdom will be radically changed when Messiah takes His throne in Jerusalem. The wolf and the lamb will lie down together. The asps won't bite, and the lions will eat straw like the cow.[2]

There will be no shortage of food anywhere in the world since in one growing season there will be more than one harvest to reap.[3] Hunger and famine will be lost concepts. The curse upon the land will be lifted, resulting in a fruitfulness that will be beyond man's imagination.[4]

The longevity of the average person will not be counted in decades, but in hundreds of years. One prophet says that if a person dies at the age of one hundred, it will be thought that his life was cut short for some reason.[5] Each family will greatly multiply as God had originally intended all families to do.

In short, the millennial reign of Messiah will be the fulfillment

---

[1] Isa. 35:5-6.
[2] Isa. 11:6-7.
[3] Amos. 9:13.
[4] Cf., Rom. 8:18-25; Acts 3:19-26.
[5] Isa. 65:20.

of God's original plan for man upon this planet.[1] Man was created to walk with and worship God, to rule over the works of God's hands, and to multiply his own family. All these things will be done the way God had intended them to be done from the very beginning. A perfect world with a perfect ruler with near perfect subjects living extraordinarily godly lives contentedly. How could it be any better than that?

All this will take place in order to teach all men what God's original intent was and how glorious His plan was for every single person from the beginning. *Every person is a member of God's family by God's own design.* There are no people left out of it, nor are only a select group of people brought into it. He created all men for the same purpose, and none of them were disqualified when they personally sinned. God made it possible for all men to return to Him and begin to serve and worship Him as Adam and Eve did in the beginning. But that choice was, is, and forever will be each man's alone.

The cross of Jesus made man's freedom to choose possible. If he makes that choice to follow Jesus, he would understand life as God explained it to him. He would also benefit from God's care and blessings. If he chooses not to come close to God but to live life on his own, he would not understand life or find fulfillment, joy, meaning, and purpose. He would be lost even though he would continue to be loved. Unfortunately, many people remain in this sad state today.

---

[1] Gen. 1:26-28.

Chapter 5

The Need to be Better at
Preparing ourselves for Judgment

The Bible is clear about some things that happen after a person dies. It is more difficult to decipher on other matters. In addition, there are a few things that the Bible is completely silent on, regardless of the intensity of our curiosity about and research into those things. One of the things that the Bible is clear on is the fact that everyone has been appointed to enter into judgment after he dies. Heb. 9:27 says,

> ". . . it is appointed for men to die once and after this comes judgment . . ."

After death, everyone will stand before God, the righteous Judge of the entire world,[1] to be judged. No one will escape either of these two appointments. There will be no second-chance reincarnations; there will be no free passes to safety beyond the Judgment Seat. This judgment awaits everyone, the so-called *believers* and *unbelievers* alike. What this judgment will cover will surprise most of the people interested in it.

Talking about a judgment which no one can avoid probably doesn't sound that familiar to most of us because we have been taught that believing in Jesus took care of that judgment for us. Consequently, the ideas that will be discussed in this chapter may be very troubling for some. We are not accustomed to even

---

[1] Gen. 18:25.

consider the possibility of being judged, right? The logic of what we have been taught goes like this: since Jesus *paid it all*[1] on the cross for all of our sins,[2] there can't be anything left for us to pay. All of the penalties resting on the sins we have committed on earth were paid by Jesus so that we cannot be held accountable for anything that we have done while on earth. Everyone wants to believe that whether it is true or not. I certainly did.

Orthodox Christianity tells us that God is completely satisfied with Jesus' payment and could not exact anything more from any believer in Jesus at the Judgment Seat. After all, the gospel that was presented to us and in which we believed is a *gospel of grace*. And who doesn't love the acrostic for grace: **G**od's **R**iches **A**t **C**hrist's **E**xpense. We have been redeemed from all costs demanded by our sins by Jesus' payment. Consequently, it is impossible for a *retributive* judgment at the Judgment Seat of God to come upon anyone who had believed in Jesus while on earth.

By this teaching, Christian orthodoxy transforms the Judgment Seat of God/Christ into *an awards ceremony* at which each person is given only blessings and benefits for the good things that he has done during his life. All the bad things, on the other hand, and the penalties attached to them, have been paid for by Jesus in His death on the cross.[3] As a result, this judgment is a place where people are praised, not punished.

What is there not to like about that view of the afterlife? If the Bible teaches such things, then that is the way it will be regardless of whether a person likes it or not. But does the Bible teach these things or have they been more *assumed* to be true due to the

---

[1] John 19:30.
[2] 1Cor. 15:3-5; 1John 4:10.
[3] John 19:30.

process of deductive thinking rather than being found in the Bible *explicitly* taught?

Remember Heb. 9:27? If believers in Jesus do not come into judgment as some claim, then Heb. 9:27 is not true because it says that everyone must come into judgment when in fact there won't be one for those who have believed in Jesus. Only the proverbial *unbeliever* (a term in desperate need of revisiting) is left to pay for his sins because he never believed in Jesus. Being without Christ, he is also without a payment to cover his sins. Being without a payment for his sins, he must endure hell until his payment has been paid in full. According to orthodox Christian teaching that means *forever* in the sense of *an eternity spent in hell.*

But there are too many verses that clearly and simply state that the one who has believed in Jesus for his forgiveness and for the gift of eternal life will indeed be judged for his wicked and worthless deeds. What follows is a list of some of those verses that can be marshalled against the idea that Christians will be excluded from a negative judgment in the afterlife.

Ecclesiastes 12:13-14: the warning of a wise King

There seems to be ample Scriptural evidence to reject the view that Christians *won't* enter into judgment at the Judgment Seat of Christ. All men, the *believer* and the *unbeliever* alike (terms that Christian orthodoxy uses that don't fit the Biblical usages for those terms), will be subjected to both a positive and a negative judgment when they stand before that Judgment Seat. Solomon, in his discussion on the correct view of life that offers meaning, purpose, and happiness to every individual who rightly lives life, said,

"The conclusion, when all has been heard, is: fear God and keep His commandments because *this applies to every person*. For God will bring *every act to judgment, everything* which is hidden, *whether it is good or evil*." (Eccl. 12:13-14, emphases mine)

The *universal scope* of Solomon's conclusion – all men -- and the *universal subject matter* of the judgment -- all deeds, the good *and* the evil – should be noted. No one stands before this Judgment Seat without giving an account for everything he has done, for the good and for the evil. This expectation continued into the NT during and after Jesus' ministry.

Acts 24:14-16: Paul's conviction *before* and *after* faith

The apostle Paul was of the same conviction both *before* he trusted in Jesus as his Messiah as well as *after* he had begun proclaiming Jesus as the Christ. He said,

"But this I admit to you that according to the Way which they call a sect I do serve the God of our fathers, *believing everything that is in accordance with the Law and that is written in the Prophets*, having a hope in God which these men cherish themselves, that there shall certainly be *a resurrection of both the righteous and the wicked*. In view of this, I also do my best to maintain always a *blameless conscience both before God and before men*. . . . And as he was discussing righteousness, self-control, and *the judgment to come*, Felix (the governor) became frightened . . .'" (Acts 24:14-16, 25, emphases and parenthesis mine)

The apostle Paul as well as the religious leaders who were accusing him all believed in *a judgment after death* based upon what they had done during their earthly lives. Solomon had warned everyone of exactly the same judgment.

But the amazing thing is that Paul expected to be judged for *everything he had done during his life* even *after* believing in Jesus. Paul did not expect Jesus' death to relieve him of the accountability that was his to answer for his evil or wicked deeds. Surely if anyone would know the effectiveness of the cross of Jesus to take away the penalties attached to personal sins, Paul would be that man. But he maintained the same conviction about the coming judgment that he had held previously as a zealous Pharisee. Obviously Paul did not believe that Jesus' death on the cross paid for his sins in a way that removed his own accountability for them at the Judgment Seat of Christ.

Rom. 14:10-12: a warning for Christians specifically

The judgment that each person must face is so complete that the apostle warns *believers* that it even includes *amoral activities*. Amoral activities are not inherently right or wrong in themselves. They may *become* wrong for any individual who participates in them without the proper faith or at an improper time. Sometimes these activities are referred to as *gray areas* or as *doubtful* (but not forbidden) *things*, or simply as *Christian liberties*.

While a Christian has the liberty to do them, he may be required to forego their performance as he seeks to minister to the weaker brother in Christ. Consequently, Paul warned Christians about misusing their liberty in Christ because God will hold them accountable for their actions when the welfare of their weaker brother in Christ is at risk. So, he said,

> "But you, why do you judge your brother? Or you again, why do you regard your brother with contempt? For *we shall all* stand before the Judgment Seat of God. For it is written, 'As I live, says the Lord, every knee shall bow to Me, and every tongue shall give praise to God.' So then *each one of us* shall give account of himself to God." (Rom. 14:10-12, emphases mine)

Christians are going to stand before the Judgment Seat of God to give an account of how they treated their brothers in Christ when amoral issues were being dealt with between them. If a Christian is more concerned about using his liberty in Christ than he is about the spiritual condition and growth of his weaker brother in Christ, he will answer for that at the Judgment Seat.

It is also to be noticed that Paul included himself in that judgment when he said, "For *we* shall *all* stand before the Judgment Seat of God," and "so then *each one of us* shall give account of himself to God." No Christian is exonerated *a priori* even when the issue to be judged is an amoral act. Believing in Jesus does not shield a person from the negative judgment that may come upon him because he has misused his Christian liberty.

2Cor. 5:10: Paul's conviction *after* believing in Jesus

In addition to these clear references to the fate of all men, those who have believed in Jesus and those who have not, we can add Paul's classic verse on this matter:

> "For *we must all* appear before the Judgment Seat of Christ that *each one* may be *recompensed for his deeds* in the body, according to what he has done, *whether good or bad*." (2Cor. 5:10, emphases mine)

Once again Paul included himself and all other Christians in the fate of standing before the Judgment Seat of Christ to give an account for everything that they have done in life. Paul is crystal clear about this when he said, "We must all appear" there! Nor was he vague about why each person will stand before that Judgment Seat. He said clearly that *we will all* stand there "to be recompensed for the deeds we have done, whether good or worthless."[1]

Christians don't get a pass. They don't get a lighter sentence because they had believed in Jesus while on earth. All Christians will be *paid back* by God (that is the meaning of *recompense* in this verse), according to divine reckoning alone, for the way in which each one has carried out, or left unfulfilled, the stewardships that were given to him to accomplish. If falling into the hands of the living God is a terrifying thing in this life,[2] we can only imagine what it will be like at the Judgment Seat.

Matt. 25:14-30 and Lk. 19:11-27: Jesus' teachings are clear

In addition to the Scriptural passages used already, we must add the two extended parables of Jesus, the parable of the talents[3] and the parable of the minas,[4] to demonstrate that there will, indeed, be a negative judgment at the Judgment Seat of Christ/God for some who have believed in Jesus. If they are judged to have been unfaithful in their stewardships, they may have to endure Jesus' just judgment upon them in the afterlife even though they may have been chastised already in this life.

In the parable of the talents as well as in the parable of the minas, the third servant of the master is not permitted to participate in the Messiah's Kingdom. Rather, he is thrown out into *the outer darkness*. This is a place where there is weeping and gnashing of teeth. If the experience of the Kingdom is described as

---

[1] The Greek text based upon the Majority tradition has *evil* instead of *worthless*, making it identical to Solomon's warning in Eccl. 12:13-14. It may be that all the religious leaders got their conviction on the final judgment from Solomon or from Daniel (Dan. 12:1-2).
[2] Heb. 10:31.
[3] Matt. 25:14-30.
[4] Lk. 19:11-27.

entering into the joy of the Messiah,[1] then the outer darkness where there is weeping and gnashing of teeth is a vastly different experience.

Consequently, the third servant in each of these parables, the one who experiences the remorse (and subsequent discipline?) in the outer darkness, cannot be one who *has entered* the Kingdom but *is not reigning* in the Kingdom. Or, as some attempt to lighten the consequence of the lazy, unfaithful servant of Jesus by differentiating between *entering* the Kingdom and *inheriting* the Kingdom, the third servant can't be one who entered the Kingdom but who did not get to serve Jesus in the Kingdom. As I have pointed out earlier, *entering* the Kingdom and *inheriting* the Kingdom are clearly used synonymously in the passage on the rich young ruler.[2] As a result, a better understanding is that all those who enter the kingdom serve Christ by ruling for Him during the Kingdom. If a person is qualified to enter, he is qualified to rule. There will be none who are simply on-lookers.

Trying to interpret the Scriptures so that *all Christians* enter the Millennial Kingdom of Messiah or so that *no Christian* is held accountable for his bad deeds at the Judgment Seat of Christ is motivated by erroneous *assumptions* (followed by an inadequate, interpretive approach to understanding the Scriptures). It all boils down to beginning one's study with the erroneous *assumption* that entrance into the kingdom and one's personal judgment at the Judgment Seat of Christ are *grace issues* when, in reality, neither one is. The *gospel of grace*, by and large, is man's creation.

It is not by grace that one enters the kingdom; it is by works done in faith. So, Jesus taught, and Matthew recorded, this point

---

[1] Matt. 25:1, 21, 23.
[2] Matt. 19:16, 23-24, 29; Mk. 10:17, 23-25, 30.

quite clearly in Matt. 7:21 which says:

> "Not everyone who *says* to Me, 'Lord, Lord,' will enter the kingdom of heaven, but he who *does* the will of My Father who is in heaven."

Three things to understand here: 1.) the term translated *does* is never used in Matthew for the exercise of a faith response without an accompanying deed or work to go with it. As a result, the verb *does* denotes a performance done in faith, not belief alone. 2.) The phrase *the will of My Father* (or the will of God) is never used as a reference for believing in either Jesus or God in Matthew's gospel. It is used consistently for the responses a person needs to give to the instructions of God (or of Jesus). 3.) These two terms (doing and the will of God) are explained in Matt. 7:24-27 quite clearly as obeying Jesus' teachings. Luke's parallel passage[1] to Matt. 7:21-27 is even more explicit since he repeats the phrase "Lord, Lord" from Matt. 7:21. For both Matthew and Luke, then, doing the will of God is obeying Jesus' teachings outlined in this sermon.

In Matthew chapters five through seven, Jesus is outlining *His gospel of the kingdom*[2] message for all of His listeners. *His gospel is a works gospel* as Jesus' whole sermon clearly demonstrates. Only by twisting the Scriptures can Jesus' message be turned into *a gospel of grace*. Hence, it ought to be thought provoking that a gospel of grace is the only gospel that we hear preached today?

Likewise, it is not by grace alone that any person is judged at the Judgment Seat of Christ/God because the judgment is not based upon what a person has believed but upon what a person has done. Like entering the kingdom of Messiah, the judgment one receives at the Judgment Seat of Christ/God is a works issue.[3]

---

[1] Lk. 6:46-49.
[2] Matt. 4:23; 5:1—7:29; 9:35; 24:13-14.
[3] 1Cor. 3:6-9, 12-15. Cf., Rev. 22:12.

If kingdom entrance is a matter of works, then one might expect the idea that wicked or evil works might keep a person from entering. This is exactly what the apostle Paul said several times: People, Christians included, who lead very sinful lives won't enter the kingdom.[1] The reason they don't enter the kingdom is that entrance is not a grace issue; rather it is based upon works. Since undergoing a final judgment has been appointed to all people,[2] there is no grace available to excuse one from this judgment.

John 5:24: an Exoneration of Christians from Judgment?

Now it is necessary to address John 5:24 in our discussion since some understand this verse as a guarantee that Christians will not enter into any negative judgment at all. All that has been said and all of the verses that have been referred to up to this point contradict this belief. Consequently, a slight twist is used to make this opinion as palatable as it can be.

When Christians stand before the Judgment Seat of Christ, it is believed by many that they will be rewarded for the good things that they had done, but they will not be held accountable for anything bad or evil that they had done. Although they may hold to the view that there is a loss of rewards for doing bad things, it should be plain to most people that a loss of a good thing (i.e., a reward) is not the same thing as being given a *pay back* or *recompense* for the bad things that they had done. *Not getting something good is not the same thing as getting something bad.*

The reason that Christians get off the hot seat is that Jesus

---

[1] 1Cor. 6:9-10; Gal. 5:19-21; Eph. 5:3-5; Col. 3:23-25. While the term used in all three passages is *inherit*, since Jesus used the term synonymously (Matt. 19:17-30) with *obtaining* or *having* or *entering* the kingdom, there is no reason to assume any difference between them.
[2] Heb. 9:27.

supposedly paid for all the bad things for them when He died on the cross so there cannot possibly be any repercussion, any *pay back* or *recompense,* for anything that they did that was worthless or just plain evil. By no stretch of the imagination, that I can reach, is being thrown into the outer darkness where there is weeping and gnashing of teeth the same thing as simply not getting something good. Being thrown into a place called the outer darkness where one experiences weeping and the gnashing of teeth looks like a bad experience that is being given for unfaithfulness. Being handed over to torturers[1] and having to receive lashes for disobedience[2] seems to demand more than simply missing out on a good thing. That is so plain that no one should miss it, right? And we must not miss the fact that the context of both of the passages just referred to discuss those who know the Lord and His will but choose not to obey it.

John 5:24 needs to be carefully examined and kept in its context (and especially kept consistent with John's use of the terms he chose to employ here). The verse, as I have translated it, reads as follows:

"Truly, truly, I am saying to you that he who *is hearing* My word and *is believing* in Him who sent Me [i.e., God the Father] *is having* eternal life and *is not coming*[3] into judgment but he *has passed* out of death into life."

In my translation of the verse, I have chosen to emphasize the *present tenses* that are used in the verse to show that John is explaining what is taking place currently as well as what took place in

---

[1] Matt. 18:21-35, noting especially vv. 34-35.
[2] Lk. 12:41-48, noting especially vv. 47-48. The reference to unbelievers in v. 46 can be and in fact ought to be translated unfaithful. Remember that there was no Greek noun for either *believer* or *unbeliever* in the Greek used in the New Testament. Those terms are created by adding an article to either a participle or an adjective.
[3] Two present tense *verbal* nouns are followed by two present tense *verbs*.

the near past so that the person was able to respond as he is in the present. What he is saying is simply this: the person who *is listening* to Jesus' teachings and *is believing* in the Father about whom He was speaking *is having* eternal life flow through him to enable him to walk in righteousness. When a person has that kind of response to Jesus' teachings, he *has already passed out of death into life*, that is, he has moved from independence from God, known as *death* in the Scriptures, to living, in this case, by the *life* that Jesus gives. If *this life* is being lived presently, then God can't presently *condemn* the actions that person is performing; He must *justify* them instead. In justifying these actions, God is declaring them to be righteous responses that meets His approval.[1]

John is saying that the person who is experiencing or having eternal life is *not separated* from God and sinning, but is *connected* to God through the shared life of His Son and is *living righteously*. But one has to move from independence or from a condition of being separated from God to a condition of dependence upon God in order to live a life that God approves.

Moreover, if he has heard of Jesus and has believed in Him, as is true in the present context, in addition to being dependent upon God by faith, he can be experiencing the *life* that Jesus gives to the obedient person. This life, called eternal life, is an abundant, overflowing experience of Jesus' wisdom, virtue, and power. *Experiencing* righteousness as it flows through you is different from being declared righteous by faith in God as the OT saints were. The difference is experiential and profound.

Nothing in the immediate context or in John's use of the terms he chose should lead the interpreter to read into the passage anything about heaven or hell or about the coming judgment each

---

[1] Gen. 15:6; Ps. 106:30-31; Rom. 2:13; Acts 13:38-39.

person must face after he dies. *The judgment referred to here is occurring presently, not in the future, and is related to God's evaluation of the life that a person is presently living.* When someone has life, that is, when someone is experiencing the eternal life that had initially been given to him freely, his responses cannot be condemned (the same word as judged). Rather than *condemn* such actions, God will always *justify* them, that is, He will always declare them righteous since they are the result of the life of His Son being manifested through the person presently *believing*. God cannot condemn what His Son is doing in and through a person who is trusting or abiding in Him.

The key to understanding John 5:24 properly, I have found, is John 3:16-21. The difficult thing to accomplish here is twofold: the task of being consistent in one's interpretation of the terms John uses and the discipline not to simply turn back to the theological meanings that have been applied to those terms. First of all, notice how similar these verses are in the big picture that they draw.

The one who *believes*	The one who . . . *believes*
Should not perish/ruin his life	*Does not come* into judgment
But *have* eternal life	*Has* eternal life

Both verses are about the prospect of living life now. Notice the italicized verbals (i.e., finite verbs and the participial phrases) are all present tenses, denoting actions being given in the present, rather than in the past or in the future. If one lives his life properly, he will not waste it (i.e., he will not perish or cause ruin to himself) nor will he reap God's disapproval (that is, he will not come into judgment) for fleshly decisions. This judgment of God upon fleshly living today may have negative consequences in this life and in the afterlife for the very same reasons: failure to carry out one's delegated stewardships in a way that is pleasing to God. But neither passage has anything to do with gaining a safe destiny after physical death or with being condemned to an eternity in the fires of hell. We must not allow Platonic thinking to seep into our exegesis and control it.

Now observe that John 3:17 begins with *for*. That term was meant to alert the reader that John is about to give a little amplification or explanation to what he had just said in verse sixteen. As an overview we can say it this way: God so intensely loved the entire world that He sent His Son to earth to die for man to free him from every hindrance to walking with Him. What Jesus did in His death, He also did in His life: He provided what man needed to live a righteous life so that he would not come under God's temporal judgment (or condemnation) now or have to answer for a wasted life when he finally gets to the Judgment Seat of Christ.

So, verse seventeen says that the Father did not send Jesus into the world to *judge* (or *condemn*) the world. Rather He sent Jesus into the world so that the world might be *saved* from the hand and intentions of wicked men who are opposed to God and His will.[1] Throughout John 3:17-21 the verb (κρινω, transliterated as krino) and the noun (κρισις, transliterated as krisis) can be translated either *judge/judgment* or *condemn/condemnation*. But the translation that you use should not flip back and forth between the two possible translations. If it does flip back and forth, you could draw the conclusion that two different phenomena are being described. There are not two different kinds of judgments or condemnations going on here; there is only one even though that one judgment might have a consequence today as well as in the future at the Judgment Seat of Christ also.

---

[1] Lk. 1:68-75; Rom. 11:11-32.

Then the apostle John gives the reader further help in verse eighteen. There the judgment (or condemnation) that he has in mind is limited to this life. He says that *the one who believes* in Jesus, (and note that this is the same wording as in John 5:24 where belief in the Father is described) is not being judged or condemned presently. Once again the present tense is used to denote a present phenomenon.

On the other hand, the person *who is* not *believing* in Jesus (note again the same wording as in John 5:24) has been judged or *condemned already*. Before the person carried out his unbelieving actions, the very responses that could ruin his life (or cause him to perish, ruining himself), God condemned what he was about to do. Because he was about to respond without believing in Jesus, that is, without trusting in Jesus' words to him, he is judged/condemned before he takes that action. Without a walk by faith, one can only sin.[1]

John verifies this interpretation when he says that the reason that the person under discussion has been presently judged or condemned is that he has not believed in the name of the unique Son of God. In other words, God judged or condemned the person under discussion because He saw that the person's actions were not going to spring from faith in Jesus. So even if he had given the right response, God would have rejected it since it did not come from faith. Faith is always necessary to please God.[2] And it is the obedience of (flowing from) faith[3] that all the apostles preached.[4]

Now we come to the climax of John's discussion with Nicodemus. John is going to give us a definition of the *judgment* or the

---

[1] Rom. 14:23. Cf., also James 4:17.
[2] Heb. 11:6.
[3] Rom. 1:5.
[4] Gal. 2:1-9.

89

condemnation that he has in mind. It is not a future judgment; it is not a condemnation to hell. Rather, it is a verdict given upon the behavior being judged or condemned. If the people love the darkness more than the light that Jesus brings (and they would do this because their deeds are evil), then they are rightly condemned or judged for their behavior. No one walking in the light is, or can be, condemned[1] because such a walk is the result of Jesus living through him. God can't condemn what He Himself or His Son is doing. Since He is altogether true, holy, and good, what He does is by definition the right thing.

The perfect tense verb in verse eighteen and the explanation by John of his point in verses nineteen through twenty-one limit the judgment being referred to as an act of God in the present. *What God sees us doing now, He either justifies or condemns.* If He justifies it, it can't receive a negative judgment, that is, some chastisement either presently or later at the Judgment Seat of Christ. If He condemns it, God would continue to be holy, righteous, and good to chastise it now in this life, if He deems it wise to do so, or wait until the Judgment Seat to chastise it. But the person who is believing God/Jesus is the person who is living as God desires him to live and, therefore, cannot be judged or condemned now or later. The person not living by faith is the one who is being condemned for not trusting in Him.

The central point that seems to be too often missed here is the fact that *it is the spiritual walk of a person that is being discussed.* It is not some presumed, initial faith in God or initial faith in Jesus (without having previously believed in God). We must remember that Jesus is talking to Nicodemus in John three and to the religious leaders in John five. Both Nicodemus and the religious

---

[1] Cf., 1John 1:7.

leaders had already believed in the God of Israel who had promised to send a Messiah to deliver them from the hand of all who hated them and establish for them their own kingdom over which their Messiah will rule. They were also trying to follow Him to the best of their understanding and ability. They were all rightly related to God although they were still capable of sinning and were doing so as they opposed Jesus, God's Messiah.

Now if all this somewhat confuses you, believe me when I say, that is understandable. It is due to our own flawed orthodox theology. You see, we wrongly talk about people being *spiritually saved* in the OT (that is, believing in God and in His Messiah, being forgiven by that faith, and possessing a promised destiny in heaven as a result). That is simply not what salvation means regardless of where you encounter the word.

We have been taught that to be *saved* one must believe in Jesus.[1] So, when we see people rejecting Jesus as Messiah in the Gospels, our theology leads us to conclude that they can't be *spiritually saved* individuals who really believe in God, who are forgiven, and who are going to heaven. Our systematization of the teaching of the Bible has managed to confuse the message completely by using seemingly very clear verses.

If the Jews could be rightly related to God through faith in Him and in His coming Messiah, then the Jews we meet in the Gospels were all rightly related to God *before* Jesus ever began His public ministry. The obvious ramification is the truth that no one in the Gospels could be coming under a *judgment* or receiving a *condemnation* that would send him to hell (according to our own orthodox, Christian theology). They would have already been saved before they either trusted in or rejected Jesus. This is the

---

[1] Acts 16:30-31.

consistent and necessary conclusion to be drawn from our own orthodox, Christian theology. Those who rejected Jesus in the Gospels did not stop believing in the God of Israel, nor did they stop believing in the Messiah that their God had promised to send them. They were rejecting Jesus because they were not certain for various reasons that He was that promised Messiah described in their sacred Scriptures.

The conclusion when all is said and done is this fact: John 5:24 cannot be used to prove that believers in Jesus can't receive a negative judgment at the Judgment Seat of Christ. It can't do that for the simple reason that it doesn't broach that issue at all. It describes God's evaluation of a person's *present* walk; it does not describe a person's *future* judgment.

Apparently, all of the people in the Gospels who were focused upon as followers of Jesus or opponents of Jesus believed in the God of Israel and in His promised Messiah. That belief, according to our own orthodox theology, requires us to understand them as *saved* (wrong term) individuals even though they were rejecting Jesus.

It should be plainly obvious to all that the term saved cannot mean what we have been taught that it means. It simply doesn't work. It is not related to forgiveness, going to heaven, or missing hell. It is, generally speaking, related to our present rescue from the sins that we have found impossible to overcome and to our future entrance into Messiah's coming kingdom. We must adjust our thinking to those facts. That will be a beginning.

Section Two

What Needs
to be Abandoned?

Chapter 6

The Need to Abandon the Idea that Conversions are Necessary

There is no need to *convert* anyone to Christianity. That is not a task that God has given to the Christian communities. Sounds like heresy from the start, doesn't it? The Greek terms that are *assumed* to refer to conversion are used thirty-five times in the Bible. Of those only six are actually translated as convert or conversion. The reader should look these verses up as I interpret them below.

In the NASB Rom. 16:5 reads: "the first convert to Christ . . ." Here the term is απαργη which is typically translated *first fruits*. This is the appropriate translation of the term in Rom. 16:5 as well. We must remember that *the message Jesus preached was a continuation of the faith of the OT*. He was not trying to start a new religion.[1] The apostle Paul certainly did not consider himself a convert, moving away from the faith that he had been raised in and trained to proclaim as a Pharisee.[2]

Again in the NASB, my translation of choice, 1Tim. 3:6 reads: "not a new convert." Here the term is νεοφυτον which actually refers to something that is "newly planted," a novice or a *neophyte*, without any indication of conversion at all. Since Paul relates this term to pride and being susceptible to the temptations of the Devil, one should understand his intention was the avoidance of beginners or immature persons in the role of leadership.

---

[1] Cf., e.g., John 5:24; 12:44.

[2] Cf., e.g., Acts 24:14-16; 26:14-23.

Ps. 51:13 reads: "and sinners will be converted to Thee." While the Septuagint uses επιστρεφω here, the context is clearly referring to turning any wayward person back to God. The basic idea of this term is "to turn about, round, or towards"[1] from one object or person towards another. Hence it describes anyone in any situation that changes the path or direction that he is traveling. *It does not necessitate a change of religious affiliations.*

David is clearly talking about influencing Israelites here. Being an Israelite himself, he would not be attempting to convert his own people with identical religious convictions to his own to another and different faith. Hence, when we see this term used, we ought not assume that such a change, that is, from one faith to another, is in view.

Matt. 18:3 reads: "unless you are converted . . ." Here στρεφω is used (without its prefix επι) of all twelve apostles who had trusted in Jesus almost two years earlier. As a result, the idea of conversion is out of the question for they would have already been converted if the old paradigm that we are familiar with were correct. *Rather, they needed a change in their perspectives and attitudes.* Jesus was certainly not saying that they needed to turn away from Him to another and different faith or religion.

John 12:40 reads: "and be converted . . ." επιστρεφω is used of *the people of God* both in the original OT context and here in John's quotation of it. Hence, it is a call for the wayward to return to God just as David had called the Israelites back in Ps. 51:13. So, once again, επιστρεφω does not mean conversion and is not a call to join a different faith or religion. Rather, it's a plea to turn back to God, a call to God's people to return to Him.

---

[1] G. Abbott-Smith, *A Manual Greek Lexicon of the New Testament*, T. & T. Clark, Edinburgh, 1937, pp. 174-75.

Acts 15:3 reads: "the conversion of the Gentiles." The noun επιστροφη, a cognate of the verb επιστρεφω, is used here. Like the verb, it denotes "a turning about (metaphorically, conversion)."[1] If we allow the apostle Paul to describe his own ministry to us, as he does in Acts 26:18-20, and if we use Acts 17 as a good example of his ministry, then the point of Paul's *conversions* was an attempt *to turn a person back to God*. It was not an invitation or requirement for a person to join either Judaism or Christianity.

There is no individual in either Testament that is described as a *convert* after he has trusted in the God of Israel or in Jesus. In fact, there is not one example of *initial faith* in God by an individual that would allow him to be considered a new convert. The concept of conversion is simply a badly drawn conclusion.

In keeping with what is being said here, the Great Commission is a call to make *disciples* for Jesus from every nation under the sun; it is not a call to make *converts* to Christianity. In many cases a disciple of Jesus can have a greater impact upon his own culture, family, and people if he were not viewed as a convert to another religion, namely, Christianity. What a person finds to be true and helpful in Jesus is more readily accepted if he is not sharing this information as a convert to another faith.

Regardless of the problem we are facing, when we are trying to help or to pray for another person, the first question that we usually ask is this: "Is he/she a Christian?" Haven't you said this yourself many times? The assumption undergirding that question is this: *being a Christian* practically guarantees that there is hope for the situation. Only the Christian can have this hope; everyone else is, more or less, without hope.

---

[1] G. Abbott-Smith, *A Manual Greek Lexicon of the New Testament*, T. & T. Clark, Edinburgh, 1937, p. 175. It is unfortunate that Abbott-Smith includes the term *conversion* in his definition since it has no Biblical support at all.

But what we should be asking is this: "Has he ever believed in Jesus at any point in the past, receiving at that moment the abundant life that Jesus offers, and does he know how to utilize the resources that he has gained through Jesus?" Our greatest problem today is that we have far too many Christians who have believed in Jesus but who don't know how to walk by faith in Him, utilizing the resources that Jesus has given to them.

Knowing the truth is a far cry from living the truth that is known. Receiving eternal life without using it can be likened to a bank account that is never drawn upon. The resources are there, but they aren't doing the owner of them any good if they aren't withdrawn and used.

The concept of trusting in Jesus is so vaguely understood and so rarely taught that it reminds me of the difficulty I had with praying for missionaries as a young pre-teen. In my Sunday school class we were taught that we should pray for our missionaries, but we really didn't know where to begin. We had never met them; we had little information about their circumstances; we didn't know what to pray for or what was God's will in the matter. No one can pray an intelligent prayer in that situation.

We don't need any more Christians like that! We need more Christians who know how to live by the life that Jesus gave them the moment they believed in Him. We need more Christians who have power, direction, and passion in their lives. We need more Christians like the first apostles who turned the world upside down even though they were uneducated men. Their secret? They had been with Jesus![1] And they knew how to continue a spiritual walk with Him after He left them physically. They changed the world they lived in because the One who had created

---

[1] Acts 4:13.

and continues to sustain the world was living through them. They didn't simply know about Jesus; they knew Him in an intimate way from personal experience.

What a tragedy it is to lead people to faith in Christ and then leave them without the proper follow-up to be grounded in Christ[1] so that they can become fruitful through Christ.[2] The great commission is about making disciples; it is not about seeking decisions from people. I wonder whether much of our evangelism today is not like a vaccination that keeps a person from a life changing relationship with the living God.

God is not Confined to Christianity

As hard as it may be for Christians to believe, God isn't just working through Christianity! There are individuals all over the world who are seeking God,[3] and He is responding to their search by revealing Himself to them,[4] sometimes in miraculous ways.

Not all people are dead in their trespasses and sins[5] simply because not everyone is constantly or repeatedly sinning.[6] And the possibility of being dead doesn't vanish when a person trusts in Christ[7] (or as the old paradigm would say: when a person becomes a new creature in Christ). Even a superficial reading of Rom. 6-8 reveals the truth that those who have believed in Jesus in the past can still die spiritually in the present.[8]

---

[1] Col. 2:6-7.
[2] John 15:1-11.
[3] Acts 17:26-27; Isa. 55:6-7.
[4] Deut. 4:25-29; 1Chron. 28:9; 2Chron. 15:2; Ps. 34:10; Jer. 29:13.
[5] Eph. 2:1.
[6] Gen. 20:1-5. You may have to check your marginal reference for the correct translation. God is saying here that a whole nation was *righteous* before Him. Abimelech was their king and a man of integrity. Yet this nation was outside God's chosen line.
[7] Cf., Rom. 6:16, 21, 23; 7:9, 10, 11.
[8] Rom. 6:16; 8:6.

But I agree that when a person is sinning, he is dead, separated from all that he could be experiencing in his relationship with God. The cross of Jesus is not only the basis for divine forgiveness, it is also the foundation for a person's freedom from indwelling sin. That freedom secures for every man the ability to choose whatever he desires, and he may desire good as well as evil. But this freedom that is his maybe relinquished by choosing to live by indwelling sin. Since it is impossible for any person not to live by faith, if one chooses to live by faith in any object other than God, he chooses to separate himself from God and from all of His resources.[1]

The Bible even challenges every person, wherever he is in the world, to praise God.[2] That is hardly a challenge from God that makes sense if some people are unable to fulfill that command. Most people understand intuitively that this picture of God, requiring from humans what they are not able to give, does not portray a very good image of God. God is working in the world apart from Christianity today. And it is necessary to be aware of that fact. Otherwise, Christians won't see people of other faiths as God sees them.

Conformity to Christianity is not Required

The world doesn't need to be like *contemporary* Christianity in order for it to be acceptable to God. In fact, the world does not have to believe all that Christians believe for it to be acceptable to God. Christianity today is not, nor was it ever intended to be, the

---

[1] Let it be clear, however, that to *choose* to live by faith doesn't make faith a choice. Faith is always a persuasion or conviction (see Acts 28:23-24; Heb. 11:1), and nothing but that according to the Scriptures. But to *walk* by one's persuasions or convictions is a choice. Every walk involves the will whether the walk is spiritual or fleshly.

[2] Cf., e.g., Ps. 66:1, 4-5; 67:1-7; 68:32; 150:6.

model for the rest of the world. When Christians are solely Biblical in their thinking, feeling, and acting, they are one expression, most probably the highest expression, of what is possible for the rest of the world. Unfortunately, we often stray from living Biblically, blocking the fact that God has spoken to the world through His Son in these last days.

If we are not making a good impression upon the rest of the world, it is due to the fact that we are not adequately expressing *the gift* that makes us different, *the gift* of extraordinary, supernatural life from Jesus. *Errant theology will not keep a person out of heaven.* Thank goodness for that because we all partake of that problem, and will, most likely, until the day we die. But a good stewardship of *the gift of life* that has been given to us will be required of us at our own judgment. Why? Because it is the difference maker, the distinguishing element between all the revelation that God has given in the past and that given in these last days through His Son.

We are no longer living in the bubble of secluded Western culture. We no longer have the time nor should we have the inclination to continue parroting what we have been taught without seriously testing each doctrine individually. We can correctly test what we have been taught only by playing the Devil's advocate with each doctrine. We do that by assuming that what we have been taught is *incorrect* unless we can find the Bible *explicitly* confirming those teachings. When I say *explicitly* confirming them, I mean that we should be able to quote chapter and verse that *explicitly* says what we have been taught. If we can't do that, we ought to consider the possibility that we have been trapped in a tangled web of *assumptions* and *conjectures* that will keep us away from the truth of the real message of the Bible. No one is *safe* in this world believing a lie, but believing a lie will not keep anyone out of heaven. No one should count terms or concepts as synonymous ideas unless the Bible *explicitly* tells us that they are.

Let me illustrate. Can you find one verse that *explicitly* says any one of the following thoughts?

> That *salvation* is a guarantee of heaven and an unbreakable promise of escaping hell?
>
> That Jesus offered Himself as the object of belief so that one could obtain *forgiveness of all* of his sins?
>
> That *justification* involves God's gift to a person of the perfect righteousness of Christ?
>
> That *eternal life* is explicitly said to be a guarantee of a heavenly destination?

And these few questions only expose the tip of a very deep ice burg that, if not taken seriously, will certainly sink the titanic of orthodox Christianity in the days ahead. Just as some of the condemned heretics in the history of the Christian church have been later exonerated, and just like some of the accepted orthodoxy of the historical church has later been overturned as heretical, the very same things are true in our day. Some who are being called heretical today will be proven to be orthodox eventually, and some of the teachings of the church that are considered orthodox and untouchable will be shown to be heretical after all.

God is ready to lead us forward, but we must be ready to throw off the baggage that we have been carrying for the last five hundred years. Having recently celebrated the five hundredth anniversary of Martin Luther nailing his ninety-five theses to the Wittenberg door, we ought to challenge every doctrine like Luther was doing. If we are willing to get rid of all errant theological baggage, we will be prepared for God's next revival. *Life* boats are made for departing sinking ships. The lazy or complacent follower of Jesus Christ is the one who is rebuked in Jesus' parables. Commendations only come to the diligently faithful.

Conversion: the Creation of a Partial God

Because we can no longer live in our little Western bubble, we must consider how our message is being received by the various cultures that we are coming into contact with daily. Is our message necessary? Is it really demanded by the Scriptures? Or is our message rooted more in tradition, namely, the conclusions of men of the past who were struggling to grasp and communicate to others the whole message of the Bible?

Most objective people cannot condone the idea that a person, who has done monstrous things in his life to other people, can evade or avoid altogether his accountability for the maliciously evil actions he performed. Whether we take Hitler as an example from modern history, or the church at Corinth as an example from Biblical days in the first century, or the Assyrians as an example from the Biblical record of the OT, most recognize that justice is not served if there is no judgment for these people. How does God balance the need for justice and the desire for grace and mercy? It is a certainty that God must explain how He does it for His ways are beyond our discovery.

God has explained it in the Bible, but because we have misunderstood that message, we have developed very distorted ideas of the balance between these two extremes. If we are honest, none of us is comfortable with the idea that there will be no personal accountability for those who have trusted in Christ. Why? Because sometimes Christians have been the most despicable and hurtful people in the world. Surely they ought to be held accountable for the repercussions of their actions and especially for all the people they have hurt in the process of blindly carrying out their self-centered and evil plans.

If the orthodox Christian view of forgiveness were true, why would anyone be motivated to share Jesus with the evil, violent peoples around the world? In fact, why would we want to share Jesus with some of our own government leaders who seem so perverted in their judgments and corrupt in their stances that no one with any sense of justice would want to get them off the hook for their destructive leadership?

When one teaching of Scripture seems to contradict another teaching, isn't it healthy to begin questioning the accuracy of both teachings? When the doctrine of forgiveness through faith in Jesus leads to the acceptance of injustice, shouldn't that pique our interest and motivate us to seek a balance between forgiveness and justice? Why would Christians be motivated to convert anyone if the conversion frees a person from the consequences of his wickedly sinful life? Many of us know exactly how Jonah felt when God asked him to preach to the Assyrians![1]

But maybe there is a balance in the Bible. Maybe we haven't seen it, I am suggesting, because we have been blinded to the real message of the Bible. God is loving and forgiving by nature, but He will by no means allow the guilty to go unpunished.[2] We assume that punishment can be administered to a forgiven person while he is in this world because we have seen it happen so many times. Should we not ask ourselves why God would be just to punish a forgiven person now, but, for some reason, He would be unjust to punish that same person after he dies? The theology that

---

[1] Jonah 3:1—4:3.
[2] Ex. 34:7.

we have adhered to for the past five hundred years has created these kinds of conundrums which have been mostly ignored because, if a correction was sought for them, it could lead to a wholesale rejection of what we have hitherto accepted as true. Who naturally wants to do that and face the eruptive consequences of rejection from our Christian friends and from the leaders within Christendom who see themselves as the protectors of our faith? The truth is a person may be forgiven and yet still have to experience a chastisement for his sin.[1] Could we have misunderstood the real purpose of forgiveness?

Conversion to What Expression of Christianity?

We've been taught to seek the conversion of the world to Christianity. But as I've been rethinking many of the propositions that I'd been taught, it occurred to me that the *convert-the –world-to-Christianity* approach has some significant problems. First, to what expression of Christianity am I supposed to convert the person? Am I supposed to convert him to Presbyterianism? Or should he be trained in the Methodist view of Christianity? Or could the Baptist view of Christianity be the correct one? Or maybe he should be converted to the Church of Christ? And since the Christian Church view is not greatly different from the Church of Christ view, maybe it should be the standard expression of Christianity to which all men should be converted.

But let's not forget about the Episcopal Church, the Nazarene Church, the Bible Churches, the Covenant Churches, the Congregational Churches, the Lutheran Churches, the Plymouth Brethren Churches, the Evangelical Free Churches, the Pentecostal and

---

[1] Cf., e.g., 2Sam. 12:13-14.

Charismatic Churches, the Quaker Churches, the Anglican Churches, and on and on we could go. If it really is our job to *convert the world*, to which expression of Christianity should we send those converts?

Answering this question exposes us to the basic reason that different Christian denominations don't, and can't, work together in many social and civic programs, but especially in *evangelistic* outreaches. They really don't believe that the other expressions of the Christian faith are true or adequate. Either something has been added or something has been omitted that makes the teachings of other denominations questionable.

But even if we are able to choose one of these more mainline expressions of Christianity, that doesn't really solve the problem. Maybe we pick one because we are the most familiar with it and thus have a natural bias toward it. Maybe we pick one because it was the preference of our parents or grandparents. But one thing we should realize: *every denomination is internally divided; some sects of the denomination believe one thing while other sects believe something different.* And these differences of opinion aren't restricted to cultural issues that may be unique to it. Some of these divisions within a denomination involve central, doctrinal issues.

Not only is the *convert-the-world* approach not practical, since no one can agree on the exact expression that should be the target group to which all the converts should be sent, the idea of converting others is both unnecessary and almost impossible to find in the Scriptures. For you who are open to these kinds of discussions, I urge you to watch when those who are ardently opposed to these ideas go to find their Biblical examples of *converts*, making sure, in the process, that the convert is being offered some spiritual blessing, like salvation or justification, that he can't have without his conversion. If you sense that they are grasping for straws, you will be correct.

Conversion, as it is viewed today, is unbiblical. God wants all people to have the life that Jesus is offering so that they can be enabled to walk more closely and consistently with Him, rejoicing in the midst of trials and sustained by the support that God is promising them. But, if possible, God wants them to bloom spiritually where they are already planted. They don't need to become a Christian, *in the contemporary sense of that term*, to have an effective ministry or an abundant spiritual life.

How great would it be if the Messianic Jews, along with all the Christians around the world, stopped trying to *convert* either the traditional Jew or the committed Muslim to the Messianic Jewish faith or to the Christian faith? In that case the person who shares Jesus would be found offering *the free gift of life* to the Jew or Muslim without requiring an adherence to either Judaism or Christianity.

The witness can explain to the Muslim, for example, lacking an understanding of his own holy book, the Quran, that the Muslim faith recognizes Jesus as a prophet. Then he could explain that Jesus desires to give to all men in whatever condition they may find themselves a wonderful spiritual life that overcomes the trials of their daily life. This life will guide, empower, and encourage them daily. It is free and can be received without becoming a Christian (i.e., converting to Christianity). The traditions and practices of Christianity have not attributed greatly to the spiritual growth of most of its members according to some of the greatest Christian leaders of the twentieth century.

So much can be averted with this simple approach which does not seek to *convert* anyone. Our task is telling people about Jesus and the extraordinary gift of abundant life that He is offering to those who trust in Him. Our task is not to *convert* people; our goal is not to make all men Christians in the contemporary sense of that concept.

God desires communion with all of His creatures. He is not requiring conformity to just one expression of faith even though He does expect that all expressions of faith respond to the revelation that He has given them initially and then to undergo the corrections that would naturally come from a study of the life and teachings of Jesus who came to explain the Father and His will.[1] There will come a time when God will expect all faiths to correct their concepts or ideas about Him.[2]

Technically, if there were no attempts at converting people, there would be fewer religious objections to a person witnessing for Jesus. Likewise, if there were no attempts at converting people, there would be far less opposition to the message from those who have no desire to leave their faith and join another. Both of these extreme situations are solved if the only thing that was being offered was a free gift to enable a person to walk more closely to the God that he presently understands in a very limited and possibly skewed way.

Is this really any different than the condition of most Christians today? Many of them have very limited and skewed views of God even after a great many years of church attendance and Christian teaching. Why would we hold the rest of the world to a different standard than the one we cling to ourselves?

Conversion is not our God-given task; discipleship is. Share the life Jesus offers. Then teach them what Jesus taught. Simple.

---

[1] John 1:18; 14:7-9; Heb. 1:3.
[2] Cf., i.e., Acts 17:22-31.

Chapter 7

The Need to Abandon the Idea that This Life is about Getting to Heaven

This is, unfortunately, the common mindset of the greatest part of Christendom today. This life, it has been concluded, is all about trying to make it to the next life safely.[1] What is the correct path that will get a person to heaven? Can one be sure that he has found that path? Is it possible to get off that path once a person has begun to travel it? Can he get back on it after he has left it? How many times can he get back on the path after leaving the path? Are works involved? Is it a grace issue alone?

These are the questions with which most Christians are completely obsessed. There is hardly anything else on the typical Christian's mind except the drive to find the path that leads to a heavenly destiny. Of course, it is the constant hope that the right path is absolutely secure forever without any potholes in it.

The most obvious problem with this approach to life is that there are numerous paths that are all claimed to be the right path by those who are currently traveling on them. As one might expect, those who are traveling on one path are fully convinced that every other path than the one they are on is the wrong path. So, if there are twelve different paths, each claiming to be the right one,

---

[1] Robert Jeffress, in his book *Not all roads lead to Heaven*, presents faith in Jesus as the only road that takes a person to heaven. See my forth-coming rebuttal of his arguments in *The Road to Heaven . . . Constructed by Men alone*. The Bible does not present *any* road to heaven. As I have shown in my book *The Grand Spiritual Assumption*, salvation is not about going to heaven. If that is true, then the message of the Bible turns out to be completely, almost incomprehensibly, different than what we have believed to be true.

then there will be eleven that are saying the path that you might be on is the wrong path. That is eleven against one. How can a person really be sure that he has found the right path in such a situation? Remember: all twelve people are basing their opinions on the Bible. So in the end it becomes a battle over the original, authoritative meaning of the Scriptures.

Since this message about finding the correct way to heaven has been practically all that most Christians have ever heard, it might appear to be an incredible statement, at first glance, to deny that the Bible actually presents such a message. "But," one might respond, "how can the Bible not be about discovering the correct path to heaven?"

> Doesn't it talk about the kingdom *of heaven*?
> Doesn't Jesus offer *eternal life*? What is that life if it isn't eternal in the heavens with God?
> Doesn't the Bible talk a lot about being *saved*? If this isn't *a salvation from hell*, what is it?
> Paul certainly spoke of having *a citizenship in heaven*? What is that describing if it isn't *an eternal residence in heaven with God*?

Additionally, there are references
> to being with Christ after death,
> to being resurrected,
> to having a heavenly Father,
> to having Jesus prepare for some living quarters in the Father's house, which is presumably in heaven,

and so on and so forth.

It seems that the conclusion is a foregone one, that is, *the Bible is warning people about a hell that is the just destination for anyone who has ever sinned regardless of how small that sin was. On the other hand, it gives instructions on how to get to heaven so that a person can live with God forever.* And since this is the message agreed upon and preached for the last five hundred years, how could it be wrong?

But, in reality, when the Bible is studied closely, the proposition that the Bible teaches everyone how to get to heaven is found to be *built upon assumption after assumption* without any direct and *explicit* statements establishing the veracity of the proposition. To say it simply: *the Bible does not tell anyone how to get to heaven, nor does it hold anyone responsible for getting there.* While that may be an enormous surprise, it should bring a huge sigh of relief as well.

If we are not responsible for finding the one and only path to heaven, then we can stop stressing over getting there. It is not our job. It is none of our business. God hasn't revealed such a path to us so we have no responsibility to find one.

And additionally, offering a path to heaven should not be our message to the world. Much less should it be the central focus of our faith. For a much more detailed discussion of all the relevant terms that are assumed to be references to heaven, see my series, *The Love of God.*[1]

Turn to your favorite Bible verses and see for yourself whether what I am saying is true or not. Do any of those verses actually explain the way to heaven without requiring the use of *assumptions ~ unproven, assumed synonyms or concepts* for heaven?

The *Kingdom of Heaven* is never used for heaven.

Eternal life is never used for heaven.

Justification is never the means of going to heaven.

---

[1] Included in the series are five books. Their titles are *The Prodigal Paradigm, Acceptable to God without being Saved?, The Grand Spiritual Assumption, Freedom through the Cross,* and *The Offer of a Second Inheritance.* These five books lay the foundation for all the points that are being suggested in this book.

Salvation is never used for being saved from hell while obtaining heaven.

Forgiveness never results in a heavenly destiny.

Where in the Bible does it say otherwise? None of the concepts mentioned above are *explicitly* tied to a promise of obtaining heaven when we die. We have constructed a theology that *assumes* rather than proves its conclusions. What does that mean? It means that *the theology that Christianity holds as orthodox is unsupportable, Biblically speaking.*

I have given sufficient evidence for a Biblical understanding of each of these terms in my series of books that lay the foundation for all that is being said here. Nevertheless, a few additional, but, hopefully, entirely adequate reasons will be given here for denying that any of these terms have anything whatsoever to do with obtaining heaven as a free gift (or of going to heaven when a person dies).

Only our ubiquitous training in America in Christian orthodoxy will raise any questions to what is being said. But we should never underestimate the power of our past training to restrict or hinder completely our progress in rethinking these matters. To reject that training after many years of holding onto it will be an evidence of the grace of God at work within the life of the researcher. Why? Because the struggle will be overwhelming for all too many.

The Kingdom of Heaven

As proof that the Kingdom of Heaven is not a reference to heaven nor to a guarantee that a person will gain a heavenly destiny, I offer the following Biblical observations.

1. It should be noted that five of the ten virgins enter the kingdom of heaven *before* they die. Hence, the kingdom could not possibly be about heaven or be in heaven. (Matt. 25:1-13)

2. Practical righteousness gets a person into the Kingdom of Heaven, not some one-time faith in God or some initial faith in Jesus (Matt. 5:20; 6:1, 33; 7:24-27). So, if the Kingdom of Heaven is the same thing as Heaven itself (or if the Kingdom of Heaven is salvation as is taught by many within orthodox Christianity), then qualifying to go to heaven cannot be a *grace* alone through *faith* alone issue. It has to include works since righteousness is always practical in the Bible. (*Imputed righteousness* is a necessary theological concept that has been developed to make orthodox Christianity work. Without it, Christian orthodoxy would be seen to be heretical.)

3. A person can have all the correct beliefs and still be outside the kingdom of heaven (Matt. 18:1-3). Admission into the kingdom of heaven is based upon character, dispositions, and works just as Jesus so clearly taught over and over throughout His ministry (Matt. 5:1—7:27; Mk. 10:17-30; Lk. 10:25-28). It is also assumed by many that this passage proves that being saved, which Christian orthodoxy *assumes* was already true of the apostles since they had believed in Jesus,[1] and entering the kingdom of heaven are not the same thing. Like so many other assumptions, this one needs to be revisited.[2] If the message of the Bible is about *the process* of walking with God, and it is, then all references to belief point in that.

---

[1] Acts 16:30-31.
[2] Cf., Matt. 19:16-17, 23-24, 25. All of Jesus' salvations are limited to this earthly sphere. None delivers a person from this sphere to a heavenly sphere. The salvation that Peter referred to here is related to obtaining entrance into Messiah's earthly kingdom.

4. Dan. 7:27 clearly states that the Messiah's kingdom is *under* the present heavens and *upon* the present earth. To take it beyond those parameters is to distort the message of the Bible.

5. Abraham, Isaac, and Jacob have to *come back from* heaven[1] *to* earth in order to participate in the kingdom of heaven.[2]

6. The prayer Jesus taught His disciples to pray asked God to bring the kingdom *to* earth.[3]

7. Elijah has to come first before the kingdom of heaven can be established.[4] This means that the kingdom of heaven cannot possibly be a current phenomenon nor a gradually developing program. It cannot begin until after Elijah himself returns to the earth to prepare the way for the Lord. Furthermore, the church cannot be involved in (i.e., inherit/enter or serve/reign) the kingdom in their mortal bodies.[5]

8. Jesus doesn't ascend His glorious throne for ruling as King over the kingdom of heaven until He returns to earth.[6] Not once is He described as being on His throne ruling today.[7]

Consequently, there are sufficient reasons to distinguish the kingdom of heaven from heaven, from salvation, or from God's work in the world today. No reference to the kingdom is a reference to heaven. The Bible is very clear on this matter; only a well-intended, but convoluted theology equates these two radically different entities.

---

[1] Matt. 22:31-32.
[2] Matt. 8:11-12.
[3] Matt. 6:10.
[4] Matt. 17:10-13.
[5] 1Cor. 15:50.
[6] Matt. 25:31.
[7] George N.H. Peters, *The Theocratic Kingdom*, 3 vols., gives 206 propositions to support the concepts listed here.

Eternal Life

The meaning of eternal life has eluded a great many people since the time it was first written down in the NT. It is still the *assumption* by the greater part of Christendom that eternal life is a promise of life with God in eternity. It usually comes as a great shock to find out that the meaning of eternal life has nothing to do with eternity or with a destiny in heaven (which is generally taken to be a synonym for eternity). What follows demonstrates the limitations of the terms translated as eternal in the Bible.

1. Eternal life is a "life"[1] that results in an experiential relationship with God.[2] Consequently, Paul can say later on that this *life* results from Christ living in us[3] by the power of God's Spirit.[4]

2. Eternal life is connected to this age[5] and to the age to come,[6] which is the millennial reign of Messiah. But it is never connected to heaven or to a promise of heaven. The age to come begins with the return of Jesus to earth and ends when His kingdom rule has ended. And that is, according to the Scriptures,[7] an *eternal* kingdom even though it has a beginning and an end.

3. Eternal life is the enablement to walk well spiritually so as to prevent the wasting of one's life now.[8]

4. Eternal life was a gift to those who already belonged to God.[9] It

---

1 John 10:10b.
2 John 17:3.
3 Gal. 2:20.
4 Eph. 3:16-17.
5 John 3:16; 5:24; 10:27-28.
6 Mk. 10:30.
7 2Pet. 1:11.
8 John 3:14-21 & 1Cor. 10:9-10; John 5:24; 10:27-28.
9 John 3:2-5; 4:10-42; 6:15-32; 17:2; Matt. 19:17-29

is not a life given to the so-called *unbeliever*; it is a regeneration of a person who is believing in and following God's new revelation being given by His Son in these last days.

5. *Eternal* in the Scriptures obviously does not describe *an existence without end* as most of us suppose. Lee Salisbury has gleaned some simple clear examples of the limitations inherent in the meaning of eternal in his article on that term.[1]

> a. The Mosaic Covenant was declared to be an *everlasting* or *eternal* covenant, but Heb. 8:7-13 speaks of it as obsolete and "ready to disappear." It is called *eternal* yet it was always God's plan to set it aside.[2]
>
> b. The Aaronic priesthood is declared to be an *everlasting* or *eternal* priesthood, but Heb. 7:7-14 explains that the Aaronic priesthood has been replaced by one modeled after Melchizedek's.
>
> c. Jonah was not in the belly of the great fish "forever" (Jonah 2:6).
>
> d. A bondslave could not serve his master "forever" (Ex. 21:6).
>
> e. God did not dwell in Solomon's temple "forever" (1Kgs. 8:13).

While others can be added to this list, the point has been made: *eternal does not have the same meaning that the English term has.* We must not use the meaning of our English term when it doesn't represent accurately the meaning of the Greek or the Hebrew terms. The Biblical limitations on the term *eternal* make it unsuitable for describing an endless existence in heaven.

---

[1] http://www.auburn.edu/~allenkc/eternityexplained.html on 11/25/17. While I have been told that Mr. Salisbury has become an atheist, his ability to be objective in his interpretation of the Scriptures far exceeds that of many theists that I know personally.
[2] Heb. 7:11-19. Cf., Jer. 31:27-34.

Justification

While most Christians don't know this, all of their hopes of a safe and secure harbor after death depend upon the accepted, orthodox, Christian teaching on justification being true. Is it true that justification is God's declaration that a safe harbor on the other side of the grave is being offered freely to the person who has trusted in Him or in His Son Jesus the Messiah. On the other hand, if the orthodox teaching on justification isn't true, there is nothing but turmoil, worry, and uncertainty left for the obsessed mind, clinging to the old paradigm of Reformed theology.

How does a person obtain *forgiveness of his sins* without which, it is generally believed, heaven would be unattainable? The answer: through God's justification.

How does a person have the *eternal penalties* that are the consequence of his sins removed? (These penalties have to be removed since they could send him to hell.) The answer: through God's justification.

How does a person obtain his *acceptable, unchanging, and permanent standing* before God? The answer: through God's justification.

How does a person get to spend *an eternity in heaven* in the presence of God? The answer: through God's justification.

How can a sinful person be declared completely righteous before God? (Another assumption = perfect righteousness is needed in order to go to heaven.) The answer: through God's justification.

As you can see, basically everything that many Christians are obsessed about is offered to them freely, according to orthodox Christianity, if they are justified by God once-for-all at the moment of initial faith in God or at the moment of initial faith in

Jesus. And yes, the concept of initial faith is vitally important for the coherence of orthodox Christianity's understanding of justification. Because of the way Reformed theology defines it, justification can only occur at initial faith in God/Jesus.

For many, if not most, justification and salvation have been treated as synonyms. If you have been justified, then you have also been saved; and if you have been saved, then you have also been justified. They are so closely intertwined with each other that they really can't be separated. If one is true of a person, then the other has to be true as well.

We will cover salvation next so we won't say anything further about it right now except this one thing: this intertwining of the two words is simply not Biblical. A person can have one without the other contrary to what orthodox Christianity says. A person can be justified but not be saved,[1] and he can be saved without being justified in the manner that orthodox Christianity says is necessary.[2] These two things do not occur together at the same time.

If justification has been correctly understood in the teachings of orthodox Christianity since the Reformation, then the following statements could *not* be true. But they are!

1. Justification is never *explicitly* connected to heaven or to going to heaven or to being a condition for heaven. Can you find a verse that says a person receives a promise or gift of heaven *by being justified*?

2. Justification is never *explicitly* connected to the righteousness of Christ. Can you find a verse that says in justification Christ's

---

[1] Gen. 15:6; Ps. 106:30-31. *Saved* is being used in the way that orthodox Christianity does.
[2] Cf., Acts. 10:1-4, 22, 34-35 with Acts 11:14.

righteousness is given to a person when he initially believes in God or in Jesus?

3. Justification is never *explicitly* connected to a person's *initial* faith in God (or in Jesus). Can you find a verse, that does not need to be massaged, that says otherwise?

4. Justification is never *explicitly* connected to the forgiveness of an eternally damnable penalty for sinning.

   Have you ever read of such a sin as an eternally damnable sin? I know the Bible talks about one, particular sin that is not forgivable in this age or in the age to come (commonly called "the unpardonable sin" in Matt. 12:31-32). But for those who have not committed that sin, can any of their other sins be eternally damnable?

   Aren't we taught that the penalty for each and every sin is eternal damnation? If that is true, then even though someone might not have committed the "unpardonable sin," he can still be sent to hell because of the penalties attached to each and every other sin he commits. Can we find such a penalty *explicitly* explained anywhere in the Scriptures?

5. Justification is never *explicitly* described as a grace alone (even with the addition of the faith element) issue. Not only may works be involved, they are *generally required* for justification to even occur (Js. 2:20-24).

In trying to set forth and defend the *supposed* Biblical concept of an *initial justification* that is obtained freely by God's grace through faith without works, a theory of two different justifications has had to be created. So, it is not only appropriate but also required for us to ask, "Are there really two different kinds of

119

justifications?" Does such a theory harmonize with Paul's teaching on justification in Rom. 4:22-25?

According to Berkhof, there is a justification of the sinner, and there is a justification of the saint (or so-called *believer*).[1] Likewise, according to Zane Hodges, there is a justification *before* God, and a justification *before* men. This approach has the advantage of being able to deflect any and all criticism of the first justification because it can always be claimed that the passage being used against it is really describing a different justification entirely.[2] This is clever, but unbiblical nonetheless.

The apostle Paul declares in Rom. 4:22-24 that not only is there just one kind of justification, *no one can be justified in any other way than the way Abraham was when God reckoned his faith for righteousness in Gen. 15:6.* The key here is that Abraham had already been walking with God *long before* this justification took place. This means that there is only one justification, and it is of the so-called *believer.* Hence, there is no such thing as a justification of a person who has no relationship with God at all whether one calls him an *unbeliever,* or an unsaved individual, or a lost person, or an unregenerate, or whatever. *God only justifies the person who is walking with Him.* In fact, that is what God justifies (i.e., declares it to be righteous): the walk of faith that a person lives in order to follow God appropriately.

When a person has no spiritual walk of faith, he can receive no justification. All justifications refer to God's approval of a person and his actions because of the faith He sees involved in his responses. *God takes a person's faith as righteousness; He reckons or*

---

[1] Berkhof, *Systematic Theology*, fourth edition, Wm . B. Eerdmans Publishing Co., Grand Rapids, Michigan; pp. 521ff.

[2] Zane C. Hodges, *Romans*, deliverance from wrath, Grace Evangelical Society, Corinth, Texas, 76210; pp. 211-12.

*accounts a person's faith **for** the righteousness He requires in the deed that is being performed.* God is not giving righteousness to a person. *In justification, God is receiving what man is offering in faith as a righteous response.* That is the clear, simple meaning of Gen. 15:6 and of the explanation of it by Paul in Rom. 3:21—4:25. *Justification is God's evaluation and approval of how life is being lived.*

Justification, then, has nothing to do with a person being qualified to go to heaven. Neither is forgiveness a necessary, inherent part of it. A person can be justified without being forgiven. Furthermore, Christ's righteousness is never given to a person in justification. Rather, in God's justifications He is signifying that He is pleased with the spiritual walk that a person is living before Him. In justification God is declaring a person to be *in the right*, that is, *righteous* if he is responding in faith. Hence, justification is God's divine declaration approving of the manner in which a person is presently living. It does not grant to a person a heavenly destiny. Nor is it a divine, once-for-all verdict of acquittal that takes away a person's sins. All such *legal overtones* are created by men rather than condoned by the Scriptures.

Salvation

It is complete conjecture to think that salvation is connected to either heaven or hell. Like the other terms already described, the terms *save* and *salvation* have nothing to do with a promise of heaven. Nor do they describe an escape from hell. The proof of this is quite simple. All one needs to do is to take out his exhaustive Bible concordance and look up every reference to *save* or *salvation*. We need only to look for *explicit* statements that clearly connect these terms with a promise or gift of a heavenly destiny.

121

While salvation can be found to be related to several issues, those issues can be broken down broadly into two categories. A person is either *saved from his sins*[1] or he is *saved from the hand of all his enemies so that he can enter the future Kingdom of Messiah in his mortal body*.[2] But neither the term save nor the term salvation is never related to heaven or to a heavenly destiny.

Forgiveness

Another astounding fact that can be gleaned from the Scriptures is that forgiveness is never described as a condition for going to heaven. It, like all the other terms already mentioned, simply has no connection to or involvement in a person's going to heaven. Rather, it is always linked to a discussion about living life now, needing forgiveness to enjoy fellowship with God as a person carries out his obedience unto the Lord.

Having sin in one's life separates him from God,[3] hinders his prayer life,[4] and puts virtues that are so desirable out of reach.[5] But never is forgiveness described as a necessary condition for going to heaven when a person dies.

Forgiveness is always linked to either coming back to God in repentance[6] or to walking with God daily.[7] If you want forgiveness, you can have it. But understand the reason that it is given. It is given in order to restore a person back to fellowship with God so he can walk with Him in love and righteousness. Forgiveness does not secure heaven for the forgiven.

---

[1] Matt. 1:21; Eph. 2:1-10.
[2] L. 1:70-71; Rom. 9-11. There is no spiritual salvation in Rom. 9-11.
[3] Isa. 52:1-2; Rom. 6:23; 1John 1:5—2:6.
[4] Ps. 66:18; John 9:31; Js. 4:1-10.
[5] Gal. 5:13-26.
[6] Mk. 1:4
[7] 1John 1:5-9.

The point that I've tried to establish in discussing all of these topics is this: the Bible really doesn't talk about heaven and hell as eternal destinies. The Bible can't talk about *eternal* destinies for the simply reason that it has no term which has the same meaning that our English term *eternal* denotes.

The Bible doesn't lay out a path for anyone to get to heaven. This appears shocking and even incredulous since the predominate belief of the Church of Jesus Christ today is that the Bible, very definitely and clearly, provides a path to heaven through belief in Jesus.[1]

All of this talk has been created by men trying to gather up the Bible into a simply message. I believe that they have missed the message and created a false one unintentionally. This is the reason we must abandon the idea that the Bible reveals a right path to heaven. Not only does the Bible not do that, but to follow such an approach also radically changes our focus, which changes our goal, which changes our message, which thwarts God's original plan for life on earth.

That original plan is for each and every man to walk with God as he carries out the stewardships that God has delegated to him. That is what life is about because that is clearly stated in the Scriptures.[2] God's plan was not changed in the slightest when Adam and Eve sinned as David plainly tells us in Psalm eight over two thousand years later. God is inviting everyone into His presence to enjoy Him daily as he carries out his stewardships in faith with faithfulness. None of these key Biblical terms have anything to do with going to heaven. We must abandon those ideas completely, and begin to focus once again on living lives that please God now.

---

[1] See my forth-coming book, *The Road to Heaven . . . Constructed by Men alone,* for a rebuttal of these ideas.
[2] Gen. 1:26, 28; Ps. 8:4-6; Eph. 2:10; Matt. 25:14-30; Lk. 19:11-27.

Chapter 8

The Need to Abandon the Idea that Traditional Orthodoxy Doesn't Promote Sin

The issue isn't whether the Bible gives its readers motivations for not sinning. Of course, it does! The issue is "Does orthodox Christianity override those motivations and promote sinful living?" That question assumes two things are true. First, a distinction should be made between what the Bible teaches and what orthodox Christianity teaches. Second, there are some teachings in orthodox Christianity that promote sinful living. To say otherwise is to spit into the wind as Tevye would say from Fiddler on the Roof.

Real life is simply too clear on this subject for there to be a substantive debate. *The religious realm is not any different than daily life routinely considered.* If the principle doesn't work in everyday life, why should we think it will work in the spiritual life?

Many of the aspects of current Christianity's orthodoxy in soteriology (theology's term for the doctrine of salvation) rest upon *the same unbiblical assumptions.*[1] We will focus upon the doctrine of eternal security as representative of all the other aspects and show how this aspect very clearly promotes sinful choices. The

---

[1] Those assumptions are that there is such a thing as *forensic* justification set forth in the Bible and that salvation is basically the flip side of justification. The Bible does not teach a once-for-all justification. It does not teach that justification is a permanent status of acquittal from all sins and their penalties. Neither does it teach that justification results in a righteous standing before God by having received Christ's own righteousness. Finally, if justification and salvation are very different issues, then for all of these reasons, the Bible will have to be read in a very different way.

orthodox Christian understanding of justification and salvation provide the basis for the doctrine of eternal security. So, if eternal security promotes sin, then those doctrines that form the foundation for eternal security do as well.

And what, you may ask, is that *unbiblical assumption* upon which all three of the before mentioned aspects of orthodox, Christian soteriology rest? It is this: *that salvation refers to going to heaven when a person dies.* That proposition is *assumed* because it cannot be proven from the Bible. As a result, our task is to demonstrate the error of what we usually hear repeated over and over within Christendom. Demonstrating this error is no small task because entrenched ideologies cannot be overturned, generally speaking, without overwhelming evidence. The issue, then, is this: "How does one disprove what is not there in the first place?" This is all pretty tricky, don't you see?

According to orthodox Christianity, if a person is saved, he is safe and secure as far as his eternal destiny is concerned. If a person is not saved, then he must spend an eternity in hell to pay for his sins. *Both of these propositions are equally unbiblical.* Saved (using orthodox Christianity's concept of being saved here) people can go to hell,[1] and unsaved (using orthodox Christianity's concept of being unsaved) people can go to heaven.[2] The Biblical basis for

---

[1] The parable of the rich man and Lazarus demonstrates that *justified* (so closely tied to *salvation* in orthodox Christianity that they can't be separated) people (Lk. 16:14ff) can go to hell. A person is saved and/or justified by faith alone in God (or in Jesus), or so we have been taught. But the rich man was sent to hell because of his choice of lifestyle, not because of what he believed or refused to believe. He had lived a self-centered lifestyle, ignoring those he could have helped with the blessings God had given him. Poor stewardship of his wealth led him to hell.

[2] None of the saints in the OT were described as saved individuals. None can be used as an example of someone being saved or being justified at initial faith in God for the simple reason that *the initial faith of no one in the OT was ever recorded for us.* There is no evidence, therefore, of anyone being saved (or justified) in the OT in the way that orthodox Christianity teaches.

these statements is simple: *the Bible never connects salvation with going to heaven.* When someone is saved, according to the Bible, he experiences a deliverance in this life, not a deliverance into an afterlife. He is delivered from trials or dangers while he lives his life upon planet earth; he is not delivered from hell into heaven after he leaves planet earth.

The argument that the doctrine of eternal security promotes sin has been around for a long time. It has also been denied by some for just about as long as it has been propagated by others. The arguments that deny that the doctrine of eternal security promotes sin use circumlocution, giving those arguments the appearance of veracity. These arguments use the Bible to list the motivations and commands God has given for not continuing in sin or in a lifestyle of sin, but for pursuing a good and righteous lifestyle. Anytime an argument uses the Bible, it is a generally very appealing to anyone who believes that the Bible is the word of God and that it gives the true perspective on life.

But there is a basic problem with this approach relative to eternal security when it is analyzed closely. Just because there are motivations offered to guide and to urge a person in one direction, it does not follow that those motivations will necessarily be effective in securing the response that is desired. In the Garden of Eden, God stated His will very clearly to Adam and Eve. Along with the statement of it, He gave them reasons for obeying it for their good.

Then Satan appeared and not only contradicted what God had said, but offered a huge enticement along with that contradiction to lead Adam and Eve in the opposite direction. "You will be like God Himself," Satan told Adam and Eve. Who doesn't want to be like God? Isn't that the highest goal that a person can ever desire? In fact, that transformation is part of God's goal for the whole human race.[1] But God's goal was supposed to be accomplished through obedience, not through disobedience.

God wanted Adam and Eve to be like Him. But He planned to accomplish that conformity through the natural maturation of a godly soul. That divine plan hasn't changed since Adam and Eve sinned. Neither Adam and Eve's sins nor those of their posterity change God's plan to mature the image of Himself planted into man's nature from the beginning of creation. All the experiences that happen to him are for the purpose of his own spiritual maturation.[2] That spiritual, transforming growth cannot be hindered if a person walks by faith[3] in the God who is leading him daily.[4]

The dilemma that we are facing here is this: what wins out in the end, the various motivations to obedience given in the Bible or the guarantee, formulated by man (wrongly using the Bible), that *no consequence of a person's disobedience will ever be allowed to come upon him regardless of what he may have done*? The answer to that question is so obvious that any detailed elaboration seems unnecessary to this writer. So, let me give you an example or two of the obvious answer to the question posed above.

Take a four to five-year-old toddler. Isn't it plain that in today's world where every parent has been frightened and intimidated against the use of any level of child discipline to correct the child's behavior that a lack of consequences is not a good thing? Every time I go out to eat, which isn't often, some child somewhere in the restaurant takes over the table where he is and

---

[1] Cf., Rom. 8:29; 2Cor. 3:18; Gal. 4:19; etc.
[2] Js. 1:2-4.
[3] Js. 1:3; 1Pet. 1:6-7.
[4] Rom. 8:14; Gal. 5:18; Eph. 3:16-17.

demands his way with a loud and persistent voice. Some children even add to that the activity by running around their table and often disrupting other tables as well. It doesn't take a village to raise a child properly; it takes obedient parents.

My wife and I have good friends, the wife of whom used to teach kindergarten. She came up with the abbreviation NHT. When she used it one evening while we were eating out with them, I asked her what do those letters stand for. She said, "NHT: No Home Training." Exactly! A child becomes a civilized human being only through thorough home training, but that almost always involves corporeal discipline along with a variety of other means of discipline as well.

And if using the toddler is not enough proof, take a teenager. Do you really see anything different in his (or her) life than what you see in the toddler's? Where there has been insufficient home training when he was younger, there is generally a plethora of mistakes, blunders, and foolish decisions made during the teenage years that follow. Now the trouble is how does the parent discipline the older person who has been given his way throughout his life? Trying to begin reining a teenager in at this point is awfully difficult because he has already been trained not to respond properly by a lack of corrective training.

Everyone has learned from experience that whenever there are no consequences given for bad behavior, it is practically impossible to realistically expect someone to do the right thing. There will always be an excuse for falling short of the desired role. The same thing is true in the spiritual realm as well. I have never known a person who hasn't admitted to me, when asked, that if he knew there would be no consequences for some inappropriate behavior, that he would be much more prone to do what he shouldn't be doing. If man thinks that God does not see what he is doing or that He will not hold him accountable for doing something inappropriate,[1] he strays as far as he can until the threat of consequences arise.

God, knowing our natures and our tendencies and the temptations that flourish around us, never promised an end to our lives that didn't include an evaluation of the behavior that we had given and appropriate consequences placed upon that behavior. As you may recall, God taught Moses, who in turn taught the Israelites, this truth nearly fourteen hundred and fifty years before the time of Christ, when He said in Ex. 34:6-7:

> "[I am] The Lord, the Lord God, compassionate and gracious, slow to anger, and abounding in lovingkindness and truth; who keeps lovingkindness for thousands, who forgives iniquity, transgression and sin; *yet He will by no means leave the guilty unpunished* . . ."

The guilty in the immediate context[2] involves those who had worshipped the golden calf while Moses had been up on the mountain communing with God and receiving from Him the ten commandments. These calf-worshipping idolaters had been previously redeemed from Egyptian slavery[3] after clearly expressing their faith in God to Moses.[4] This was the same faith that had brought their forefathers down to Egypt in the first place. God had told them to go; they obeyed and went. We have no adequate reason to believe that the faith of the forefathers was not passed on to all the generations after them.

When the apostle John said that *Jesus paid it all,* he was setting before his readers a phenomenal truth. *But what He paid for was*

---

[1] Isa. 40:27.
[2] Ex. 32:30-35.
[3] Ex. 15:13, 16.
[4] Ex. 4:31.

not an escape from His just evaluation of their behavior. Rather, He paid all that was necessary for an opportunity to live life in a way that would be pleasing to God while that life was being lived upon this earth. Jesus paid it all so that every person can walk in righteousness.[1] To the extent that a person chooses not to walk righteously, to that same extent he may experience the discipline of the Lord.[2] If we are not spiritually disciplined in this life, there may be consequences to bear in the afterlife because the apostle Paul clearly said that God will pay each person back for every worthless or evil deed he has committed.[3] His grace provides all we need now; His justice will evaluate whether we allowed His grace to train us in living appropriately upon earth.[4] But His grace does not set aside His coming just judgment.

Jesus did not pay for your sinful lifestyle so that you can remain in it without having to give an account for it. He paid for all of your sins so that you can return now to God to live pleasingly before Him. *There is no payment provided at the cross that will be applied to the Judgment Seat of Christ.* Once there, each person is on his own to give an account of himself for the life he lived.

If you have a tendency to tell little white lies, or to be impatient, or to become angry over the circumstances that God has deemed wise to bring into your life, or to be anxious or fearful about every unknown in life (or about your past life so that those past situations control your responses today), or if there is anything else that God has given a direct command concerning, understand that those deeds (responses) will be judged and an appropriate consequence will be assigned to you in the afterlife.

---

[1] 1Pet. 2:24-25.
[2] Heb. 12:4-11.
[3] 2Cor. 5:10.
[4] Cf., Tit. 2:11-15.

No one, according to Heb. 9:27, escapes this judgment. Every deed performed will receive an evaluation and recompense from God according to both the apostle Paul and King Solomon. If this prospect does not bring a whole lot of sobriety, along with a fear of God, into everyone's life, then Paul would say[1] that person is not seeing the matter clearly. The popular idea of a *death-bed conversion* wiping away all of a person's sins and the penalties attached to them should not be counted upon. Such an idea is unbiblical on so many levels. What we have done, we will be held accountable for having done. Pure and simple.

So, now is the day of salvation! If you are in a far country, spiritually speaking, now is the time to repent and return to God for the forgiveness of your sins so that you can walk with the God who so dearly loves you. God's judgment upon each person will be beyond anyone's understanding because there will be a mixture of justice, grace, and mercy, along with other traits that we have never or seldom considered. While the judgment will be appropriate, it may be quite different than the typical black-and-white, "believed in Jesus" versus "did not believe in Jesus" scenario that we have so often heard. God understands where you have come from, what you have endured, and what you are like down deep where it counts. When all is said and done, we will all understand that His chastisements are always lovingly applied and remedially intended.

---

[1] 2Cor. 5:11; Acts 24:14-16, 25.

www.ingramcontent.com/pod-product-compliance
Lightning Source LLC
Chambersburg PA
CBHW060357090426
42734CB00011B/2169